PHYSICAL EDUCATION FOR
HANDICAPPED CHILDREN

HUMAN HORIZONS SERIES

PHYSICAL EDUCATION FOR HANDICAPPED CHILDREN

Sarah J. George & Brian Hart

A CONDOR BOOK
SOUVENIR PRESS (E & A) LTD

ISBN 0 285 64979 5 casebound
ISBN 0 285 64984 1 paperback

Photoset and printed in Great Britain by
Photobooks (Bristol) Ltd

Contents

Acknowledgements

With grateful thanks to Pat without whom this book would never have been written, to the staff and children of the Cedar School and to Sue. Also to Macmillan Publishing Company, Inc., New York, for permission to quote three short passages from *Recreation for the Physically Handicapped* by Janet Pomeroy, © 1964 Janet Pomeroy.

1 Physical Education and the Handicapped Child

Introduction

The Cedar School is a day school for physically handicapped children aged between three and 17 years. They have a great variety of handicaps and therefore a wide ability range. At present, there is a predominance of children with spina bifida, but this emphasis could obviously change and the system would then have to be adapted accordingly.

The school is run by the Hampshire Education Authority and the staff comprises teachers, physiotherapists, occupational therapists, nurses, speech therapists and care staff. The roll at present is approximately 80 children.

Sarah George is a physiotherapist at the school, one of her functions being maintenance physiotherapy. This involves helping the children keep physically fit to their maximum potential. Brian Hart is a teacher, and one of his functions is to teach Physical Education throughout the school. He feels very strongly that sport has as great an importance to the disabled as to the able-bodied, and can give as much enjoyment.

As they worked, each in their separate fields, Sarah and Brian realised that they were both doing the same things with similar ultimate aims. From their own point of view they were unnecessarily duplicating work. Moreover, if they looked at the pupils' point of view, they realised that by working together the benefits to them could be threefold:

a   If it were possible to incorporate the physiotherapy with the PE, a lot of time could be saved (for children would not be taken out of academic classes for physio).
b   Physiotherapy in the guise of games would be more interesting for the children.
c   Such a 'co-operative system' would stop children wasting time and playing one member of staff off against another ('Can't do my maths now, got to go to physio!').

They therefore decided to amalgamate and together built up a programme in which the physio was incorporated into the games lesson. As time went on the value of the 'Team Approach' was appreciated and gradually more staff, such as the nurses and the occupational therapists, came to be involved. It is the purpose of this book to explain the Cedar School system for the benefit of others who would like to adapt their own programmes in a similar way.

What contribution can sport and physical recreation make to the life of the physically handicapped child?
In order to make a true assessment of the value of these activities it is essential that our interpretation of 'sport and physical recreation' be understood.

Sport and physical recreation can cover any physical activity or game which gives pleasure and relaxation. In its widest sense, this means any activity which requires some form of physical movement. It could range from an arduous game of wheelchair basket-ball to a sedentary game of chess (for to some physically handicapped children the action of moving a pawn on a chess-board can be a major physical feat). However, we are here particularly interested in 'active' games and sports, such as canoeing, athletics and fencing, rather than the 'fireside' games or hobbies, such as chess or ludo.

First of all, let's consider the aims and objectives of sport and physical recreation. The most important objective is *ENJOY-MENT*! This applies to anyone, whether he be physically handicapped, able bodied or mentally handicapped. If the game does not bring joy and pleasure to the participant, what is the point in continuing the game? It must be fun. Once the fun disappears the value of the game, in every other respect, is progressively diminished.

Through enjoyment other benefits are derived: physical development and fitness, mental development, social integration, emotional experience and a sense of achievement. The importance to anyone of physical well-being is, firstly, that it makes one feel good. Moreover, it stimulates the body processes. One is therefore better able to think, to be aware of and to appreciate what is going on around one. It leads to a fuller life because one has the physical stamina to cope with everyday situations. For the physically handicapped child this is particularly important, because if he remains immobile all day long, his weight will increase and movement of any sort will grow progressively harder to achieve. One paraplegic young man we spoke to said, 'I must keep fit, so that I can keep my independence. Keeping my arms strong means that I can lift myself with relative ease from my wheelchair to my car.'

Moreover, the physically handicapped child who has been overprotected or who might have spent a long time in hospital, has missed a great deal of 'physical experience'. He has missed play opportunities and often contact with other children has been overlooked. Perhaps he has never fallen over or bumped his head. He may never have been in a potentially 'dangerous' situation and is therefore unaware of the implications. Never having learnt in progressive stages the inherent pitfalls of every situation, as the average child does, he is either going to be petrified, or at great risk of serious injury, when, as invariably must happen, he is left to cope on his own. Sport and physical recreation can provide situations where he can make up for this lack of experience.

The physically handicapped child needs to learn to reason, to make judgments, to think for himself, in the same way as any other child. Sport and physical recreation can help him to do this in a number of ways. Learning the rules of games and how to apply them, learning to referee, umpire or score, gives him practice in instant decision making. Also, as Pomeroy* says: 'The development and use of mental powers is often the primary means of preventing excessive boredom in the life of handicapped persons.'

Such outdoor pursuits as camping, orienteering, sailing and canoeing will help him to be more aware of his surroundings. His awareness could have far-reaching results in stimulating other hobbies – perhaps an interest in birds or flowers. Moreover, these activities help him to solve small but important everyday problems. Each problem solved means a step nearer to mental maturity.

The physically handicapped child, like any other child, must learn to control his emotions: he must learn to accept and be

* Pomeroy, Janet, *Recreation for the Physically Handicapped*, Macmillan Publishing Company, New York, 1964.

accepted by his classmates, family and the society in which he lives.

Physical recreation and sport can help the child to control these emotions – through the discipline of team games. There is the frustration of missing the winning shot, and the even greater frustration of seeing someone else miss it. The disappointment of losing, the joy of winning, learning to accept defeat and victory with the same degree of sportsmanship. All these emotions are experienced in team games. If the player can learn to control them he will have made great steps towards emotional maturity.

When a child fails to complete a task, self discipline is needed to try again. For instance, the physically handicapped archer who cannot seem to hit the target; with constant effort, good coaching, and self discipline he will eventually succeed, and his efforts will be rewarded with the sense of achievement that success will bring. Through the effort and the ultimate sense of achievement an important lesson is learnt.

In learning to play together with others according to set rules, the physically handicapped child is in a way making up the ground he has lost through being so often deprived of early play opportunities. Not only is he learning *to play* but he is learning *to play with others*.

Thus, once a child has learnt to play team games (by team games we do not merely mean football or basketball, but any game involving sides with more than one person) in addition to the skills he will unconsciously acquire, he will also find it easier to make positive relationships.

So often the physically handicapped child is an 'under achiever' in his life. Sport and physical recreation can remedy this situation and give him a sense of achievement, either as one of a group or as an individual. To score the winning goal in a wheelchair football match or experience the thrill of riding your first horse are but two examples. As Pomeroy* comments: 'Much of the value of group activity for the handicapped is due to the fact that achievement on the part of the group is shared by individual members, some of whom may not be able to gain individual success.'

However, the physically handicapped child will never realise

* Pomeroy, *op. cit.*

the fullest possible development that sport and physical recreation can offer if its provision is unenlightened or shortsighted. In the final analysis, everything falls back on the teacher, physiotherapist, occupational therapist, youth club leader, recreation organiser, parent, local education authority, national authority or any other individual or body which is involved with the organisation of sport and physical recreation. The personality and effectiveness of these people are then a critical factor in bringing about the realisation of the full potential of a physically handicapped child. The leader must be aware of each individual's capabilities and work at the level and pace of each. If, through lack of understanding, he expects too much and pushes too hard, his pupil will probably be discouraged and give up. However, if the pupil is not stimulated enough, he will again lose interest.

Perhaps the greatest contribution that sport and physical recreation can offer the disabled child is social contact. For through such shared activity he is not only able to mix with others who are handicapped, but he also has the opportunity of mixing with the able bodied. The enlightened sports centre manager can do a lot to help integrate disabled children and adults into the community, if he is willing to open his facilities to *all* sectors, including the physically handicapped. But, as Janet Pomeroy* points out: 'Unfortunately recreation leaders who are trained in general community recreation tend to believe that they are not qualified to work with such persons. In reality, however, they may be the most desirable leaders to be so doing. Although working in recreation with persons who are truly ill requires specialised training, it does not follow that the community recreation leader needs to be medically orientated to work successfully with physically handicapped persons who are well.'

Thus sport and physical recreation have a great deal to offer the physically handicapped child. This is borne out by a conversation with a disabled friend who said, 'At 17 I became disabled. It wasn't until 10 years later, when I found out about and joined a sports club for the disabled that life got a meaning again for me.' It was not merely the sport which gave this woman a new lease of life, but the companionship she found

* Pomeroy, *op. cit.*

while participating in the sport, which gave her a feeling of belonging. Hence sport and physical recreation not only improve the physical well-being of the handicapped child but also give him a richer life and help him to adjust socially and psychologically to his handicap. Above all, sport and physical recreation give him the joy of participating with others.

In discussing sport and physical recreation, we may have given the impression that only certain children with limited handicaps can benefit from it. So at this point we would emphasise that all children, no matter how handicapped, have some potential for physical movement. A child may not be able to move in an orthodox manner, but that does not matter so long as he is encouraged to develop any possible movement of which he is capable. One boy at the Cedar School was confined to an electric wheelchair for the majority of his activities. He took part in the circuit (see page 39) with the rest of his class, but had great difficulty in moving from one activity to the next, due to extensor thrust in his legs and flexor spasms of his arms. However we found he could roll to one side quite expertly and when he couldn't persuade anyone to carry him, he had to resort to this method to get around. He can now complete the floor exercises as efficiently as anyone else. He used to believe that he could not move unaided, but he now knows that over short distances he can move by himself, using a very efficient amphibian creep. This has given him a great sense of achievement.

For guidance, below are some normal developmental stages. For example, kicking is followed by reciprocal kicking. In the same way:

rolling

↓

the beginnings of sitting/head control

↓

pushing up from sitting

↓

bouncing

↓

the beginnings of balancing

↓

standing by leaning

↓

steps around the furniture

↓

waddling

↓

running

↓

kicking a ball

↓

climbing

↓

jumping

↓

stair climbing

Similarly the hands begin by:

reflex grasping

↓

reaching

↓

finger play

↓

shaking a toy

releasing

↓

passing article from hand to hand

↓

grasping with thumb and index finger

↓

holding toys in each hand

↓

starting to build

↓

drinking

↓

throwing ball

↓

catching ball

↓

bouncing ball

Obviously every child will have variations on this theme but it may be a useful guide as to the most common sequence.

Although there is a general norm for the developmental stages in the acquisition of motor skills, it must be emphasised that physical age is irrelevant when dealing with handicapped children. This is because their physical development is very often delayed for a variety of reasons, such as long periods of hospitalisation, negative attitudes, lack of experience, over-protective parents, and so on. On the other hand, it cannot be emphasised too strongly that mental age is of the utmost importance. Although the object of a task is the same with a three-year-old as with a 12-year-old, the approach must be different. Nursery rhyme games which will appeal to a toddler will insult a 12-year-old. The approach when teaching any skill must be adapted to each individual, so that he wants to learn because he finds the task attractive.

Experience of all kinds is vital to the handicapped child and the more varied the experience the better. Before one says, 'This child can't because . . .' one must think, 'Is there a way?' A simple example here is the wheelchair child who 'cannot play football because he cannot kick the ball'. By pretending his chair is his legs, he will probably manage well and he will certainly be lethal in a tackle. One must always try every possible way and break each task down to its simplest form.

For example, a little boy is unable to catch the cricket ball his father throws to him. If dad just gives up, both child and parent become angry and frustrated. There is yet another failure to cope with. But if dad stops and thinks, he may then try with a softer tennis ball – perhaps with equally dismal results. But if one breaks down the task of catching a ball, the skill required to complete it is enormous. A child must be able to bring his hands together, see the object flying towards him, judge its speed so that he is aware of when it is going to reach him, and get his trunk balanced so that his arms are free to move towards the ball. Not so easy a task when looked at in this way!

Reduced to the basics, can the child in question get his hands together? If not, this must be your first aim. Begin with large articles which are brightly coloured or make rattly noises. Get the child sitting comfortably, really well supported so that he is able to concentrate totally on his hands. (Bean bag chairs are useful supports for such an activity). Get him to clap in time to music, holding things with both hands. From this basic framework, the skill of catching can be developed. Firstly, use a large brightly coloured ball, like a beach-ball. Use the voice as a stimulant and guide, 'One, two, three . . . catch.' When the child can catch a beach-ball, use a progressively smaller ball until the child can eventually catch the tennis ball.

If your child cannot do a task, do it yourself and analyse what you have to be able to do to complete it. Reduce it to its simplest form and gradually build it up until your child achieves the original task. Very often other children can help.

It is so easy to park a handicapped child in a corner and just let him watch. It is very often extremely difficult to see *the child* behind his handicap, for one can be so overwhelmed by or afraid of the handicap that one forgets the child. However, as soon as one remembers that a handicapped child is first and foremost *a child*, one will realise that, like all children, he will want to be involved, to be part of the proceedings, to try, to be encouraged, to be accepted and to achieve.

As with all children this involvement begins in the family with his parents and siblings. If he takes his rightful place within the family and is not the focal point; if he is treated 'like the rest', all within their own limitations, a physically handicapped child has a better chance of developing a good self image and will therefore set off into the outside world with greater confidence. Although this is true for every child, it is even more important with a handicapped child, for he has the added difficulty of his handicap.

As he grows older the handicapped child has the same needs as his able-bodied friend, to be accepted into and made part of his community. For this reason we feel it is very important to encourage handicapped children to mix as much as possible with able-bodied children. The earlier they get used to one another, the easier it is for all. Four-year-olds accept; they do not have the inhibitions and fears of the 10-year-old. Handicapped and able-bodied children should be encouraged to play together from an early age, so that integration into the community becomes a natural progression rather than a hurdle to overcome.

2 Handicaps and their Problems

There are many types of handicap. The following are the ones most often found in special schools for physically handicapped children. The most common at the time of writing is spina bifida.

1 Spina Bifida

This is a disorder caused by a malformation of the spinal column, which exposes the spinal cord and nerves at that level and prevents them from functioning normally. The child may present with hydrocephalus which is a build-up of cerebro-spinal fluid in the brain and spinal cord, possibly causing a degree of brain damage. Hydrocephalus is often treated with a valve which syphons the fluid away into the heart.

a *Watchpoints*

There is a lack of, or alteration in, sensation. This is usually in the lower limbs and the lower half of the trunk, but it varies with each child. It is therefore necessary to:

(i)   Avoid pressure, since any prolonged pressure may lead to sores.

(ii)   Be wary of burns. These may be caused by exposure to or contact with extreme heat or cold, or by friction. Radiators are especially dangerous.

(iii)   Use safe apparatus, for cuts, breaks and bruises may all occur with the child remaining totally oblivious. It is therefore essential that he wears sensible shoes to protect his feet.

b *Valves*

To date, a valve has not been made which will 'grow with' the child. Thus care should be taken to ensure that the valve is not overstretched in a growing child. As the valve is situated in the blood vessel which goes from the head to the heart it is wise to avoid 'head-over-heels'.

c *Appliances*

All staff should be aware of the children who have urinary appliances. Thus, if an appliance should become detached during an energetic exercise, the child can be sent to deal with the problem with the minimum of fuss. With some children it is possible to tell when the bag needs emptying. It may save a lot of problems if a gentle hint is dropped! (We deliberately say 'drop a hint', rather than 'tell the child to empty his bag', because we feel that, providing the child is old enough, the responsibility for his bag is *his* and not the teacher's.) Ideally the school nurses should devise individual programmes, involving the parents and any who work with the child, to teach him the care of his own appliance.

d   *Calipers*

At present calipers remain heavy and bulky. At the Cedar School those children who do not walk all the time (using thoracic or pelvic band calipers) may use a wheelchair for games. As they get older and more responsible they are given the choice either to wear calipers or to sit in a wheelchair – with or without calipers – provided there is no medical need for them to wear them all the time. Certain children prefer to wear their calipers for protection during games even when in a wheelchair, as many of them have fairly brittle bones. If this is a problem discuss it with the child's orthopaedic consultant.

e   *'Cocktail Party Chatter'*

These children have a skilful knack of covering up a problem or avoiding a task by talking their way out of it! Think hard before you acquiesce!

f   *Perceptual Problems*

Children with spina bifida are often not aware of their body in relation to space, nor do they see it as others see it. It is therefore important to ensure that all your instructions can be clearly understood. For example, does the child appreciate the meaning of 'line up one behind the other'?

g   *Self Care*

One must remember that a totally protected child will never have any awareness of the dangers to which he may be exposing himself. There are many things that we take for granted that a child with spina bifida must be taught. For example, he must be taught to keep away from radiators because they can seriously burn him. He must be taught to check himself regularly for sores and to drink plenty to keep his kidneys functioning well.

Aims

Very generally therefore, one's aims with a child with spina bifida will be:

   (i)   To strengthen the trunk muscles and those of the arms, shoulder girdle and whatever leg power is available.

   (ii)   To retrain perception when this proves to be part of the handicap.

   (iii)   To improve balance and co-ordination. (For example, in a game of basketball both skills must be highly developed).

   (iv)   To improve wheelchair or walking skills.

2   Cerebral Palsy

This is a non-progressive, but not unchanging disorder of the nervous system. Each child with this very broad label will be very different. There are, however, fairly clearly defined types:

a   *Spastic Quadriplegic*

A child with this type is generally described as having 'poverty of movement'.

Watchpoints

   (i)   As he has difficulty in altering his own posture, he is liable to develop deformities and contractures if his position is not regularly altered. He must therefore be encouraged to stretch and move as much as possible. For a specific task, he will be able to perform well if he is in a good stable position to begin with.

   (ii)   He has perceptual problems. He does not perceive the world as the average person does.

b   *Hemiplegic*

This child is generally described as having one side of the body affected.

Watchpoints

   (i)   Some children will have problems in relating to the affected side at all. For example they will draw half a clock face or will walk into something because they are not aware that one half of their body exists. They should therefore be encouraged, from as early an age as possible, to use the affected side, and to take weight on it. For example, they should be encouraged to use both hands to push themselves up in order to stimulate the receptors in the affected side.

   (ii)   Some children have difficulty in relaxing the affected side. Gentle rhythmical exercise (eg shaking) may help to overcome this.

c *Athetoid*

This child is generally described as performing uncontrolled writhing movements of the limbs, head and trunk.

Watchpoints

(i)   This child will have a problem of balance.

(ii)   Concentration will be difficult.

(iii) Speech and hearing may be impaired.

However, it must be emphasised that many of these children are intelligent and, though very physically unstable, they have the drive and potential to walk alone.

d *Ataxic Athetoid*

This child generally has the same symptoms as the athetoid child with increased unsteadiness and asymmetry.

Watchpoints

(i)   Balance is a problem.

(ii)   Co-ordination is difficult.

(iii) Speech is impaired.

However, these children are often well motivated. Thus, though they are very physically unstable, they will often succeed in a task on account of their perseverance.

e *Spastic Diplegic*

This child is generally described as having the legs more affected than the arms.

Watchpoints

(i)   This child tends to use the arms at the expense of the legs. It is therefore important to encourage the use of *both* arms and legs.

(ii)   The disability of the trunk will cause a lot of problems of balance and co-ordination.

(iii)   This child has perceptual problems as he is not aware of his body as it really is, either in relation to space or as others see him.

f *Bi-lateral Hemiplegic*

This child is generally described as having the whole body affected, although the arms tend to be more affected than the legs.

Watchpoints

(i)   Balance is difficult.

(ii)   Co-ordination is a problem.

(iii) There is the problem of asymmetry, ie it is very difficult for him to do anything which is symmetrical.

g *'Locked in syndrome'*
This is really a self-explanatory title and these children are thus usually very heavily handicapped.
Watchpoints
(i) They often have the added problem of impaired hearing.
(ii) Symmetrical activities should be encouraged.
Thus with all children with cerebral palsy one has the same broad based aims. These are to improve
(i) Balance
(ii) Co-ordination
(iii) Concentration
Each child should be involved at his ability level. However, this level should be reviewed constantly by the team.

3 Muscular Dystrophy

a *Duchenne Muscular Dystrophy*
This is a condition which mainly affects boys. Girls are the carriers. It is a progressive and self limiting condition. The usual progression is:
(i) Walking until early adolescence.
(ii) Using a self propelling wheelchair.
(iii) Using an electric wheelchair.
Watchpoints
(i) At each stage of the disease, it is important that the child is kept as mobile as possible, within his fatigue limits. Swimming in a heated pool is stimulating. Exercises are very often possible if slightly modified; for example, a beach ball can be used instead of the relatively heavy basketball.
b *Becker Muscular Dystrophy*
This is a very similar type of muscular dystrophy but it is usually diagnosed at a later chronological age and the boys usually stay on their feet longer.
Watchpoint
(i) It is important to learn how to lift correctly – see lifting notes at the end of the book.

4 Haemophilia

This is another genetically bound disease, which mainly affects boys who, due to a lack of the blood's clotting agent, have great problems in stopping any bleeding.

Watchpoints

(i)   Bruising is a real problem, since a bruise is a contained bleed. Thus any form of contact sports should be avoided.

(ii)   Twisting sharply at any joint, especially weight bearing, will cause bleeding into that joint. Repeated bleeding into a joint wears away the joint's tough protective cartilage, pre-disposing the boy to many problems and to pain. Sports that involve twisting sharply (eg football) should be avoided.

(iii)   Should the boy have a bleed whilst in your care, and this may happen for no apparent reason, all weight should be taken off the joint. If the child is not old enough to treat himself, medical advice should be sought. If the child should slightly cut his finger, the two edges should be squeezed together.

5   Spinal Muscular Atrophy

This is a disease which affects the anterior horn cells of the spinal cord. The children with this condition are usually 'floppy' and have varying degrees of power in the trunk and limbs.

Watchpoints

(i)   Those children who have weak chest muscles are prone to chest infections.

(ii)   These children may develop contractures and deformities if they are not encouraged to stretch and move freely around the floor, swimming pool or trampoline.

(iii)   There is a danger of dislocating the shoulders if the child is lifted incorrectly (see the advice on lifting at the end of the book).

(iv)   Scoliosis (curvature of the spine) may result if bilateral activities are not encouraged.

6   Osteogenesis Imperfecta (Brittle Bones)

These children have bones which fracture easily.

Watchpoints

(i)   The bones easily fracture, therefore contact sports should be avoided.

(ii)   These children often spend an unnecessarily long time away from school with fractures in plaster. This is especially true when they go to normal schools. There is usually no reason why they should not return to school with the limb in plaster. If there is any doubt the orthopaedic consultant will give advice so that schooling can be safely organised.

(iii) Swimming may well ensure a gradual return to full activity after a fracture, as this medium supports the body, allowing it to exercise to its maximum potential.

7 Asthma

Children who suffer from asthma are pre-disposed to spasms which restrict the free passage of air in and out of the lungs.

Watchpoints

(i) The attacks may be triggered off by something specific. This should be known and avoided if advised.

(ii) For those children who seem to have attacks following exercise, a specific table of graduated exercises may have to be incorporated in the routine games programme. (See paper *Exercise Training for Children with Asthma*, Mallinson, Burgess, Cockroft and David. Chartered Society of Physiotherapy, April 1981.)

If a child has an asthma attack whilst in your care, relaxation and reassurance are of utmost importance. For specific treatment, each child may well be on different medication. It is therefore essential to check on this beforehand, so that you are prepared.

8 Epilepsy

This is a recurring disturbance in cerebral activity with a sudden flood of unchecked activity which causes a seizure. This may be major or minor; if the former, the child may lose consciousness.

Watchpoints

(i) Be prepared. If you are in charge of a group, it is essential that you are aware of anyone in the group who suffers from epilepsy. Similarly all your helpers, and the other children in the group, should be aware and know how to put the affected child into a semi-prone position and to remove any potentially dangerous objects. However, these children are usually well controlled by drug therapy and special precautions are rarely necessary.

(ii) Swimming may be unwise as the shimmer of the lights on the water may trigger off an attack and cause possible water inhalation and subsequent drowning. In fact, any epileptic may have a convulsion in the pool. Medical advice and permission should be sought prior to taking this child swimming.

(iii) Should a major attack occur, you should ensure that the child is not in any danger of injury from nearby furniture, apparatus or people. When he recovers consciousness, the child should be treated with gentle reassurance and allowed to rest. Do not make a spectacle of him and don't panic. A minor attack may well pass unnoticed or be registered only as a rather 'blank spell'.

9 Connective Tissue Disorders

This is rather a vague umbrella term for a group of children for whom, often, no other diagnosis can be made.

Watchpoints

(i) The child may well have problems with the tissues contracting, causing pain and deformities.

(ii) On the other hand the tissues may become lax and also cause pain and deformities.

(iii) As with any handicapped child, it is vital to liaise with the medical staff involved so that you can acquire a general picture of the child. Once you have this you can decide on a practical common aim. You must, however, be aware of any particular problem, eg any cardiac involvement, before you devise a programme.

General Watchpoints

If you have a physically handicapped child in your care, there are some general rules which may prove helpful.

A teacher in a special school can relatively easily obtain information about the children in his care. He should also have easy access to the various other interested specialists, such as physiotherapists, occupational therapists and nurses. The teacher in the normal school is faced with a much bigger problem. His information may well be limited to the child's name and the diagnosis of the child's condition, combined with a marked awareness of his own lack of knowledge. A teacher's natural reaction is to protect and to 'play it safe', but with increasing insight he will become aware of the child's potential and be able to plan a realistic programme. The physically handicapped child who is not stretched to his maximum potential, either physically or academically, may as a result fail in the 'normal' school system. Consequently he may require to be transferred to the special school. Such a transfer can be as disastrous for him as failing in the normal school, since he may then find himself behind his peer groups, especially in their basic independence skills. This situation can be very damaging to a physically handicapped child and some of them never seem able to make up the lost ground.

So if you are a teacher in a normal school, who has a physically handicapped child in your class, it is essential that you find out as much as you can about the child's medical history, his physical potential and his academic capabilities. You should be able to obtain a lot of relevant information if you go and meet the staff of his previous school and discuss the child with them. The referring authorities should have documented the child on special education forms which may provide a lead. The physiotherapy and occupational therapy departments of your local hospital may be able to put you in touch with their community representatives for the child's area or for that of the school. These skilled professionals should be able to advise and help you with most of your problems.

As a teacher confronted with the problem of a physically handicapped child in your class you should ask yourself:

1 How independent is the child able to be?
    a Are the different school areas (playground, library, classrooms, chemistry laboratory, etc.) accessible to him?
    b Is he able to cope alone in the toilet?
    c Is he allowed the same freedom as the other children?
    d Do I, as his teacher, treat him very differently from the other children?
    e Do I make demands of him as I do of other children?
    f Do I want him in my class?
2 Does he follow the normal school curriculum?
    a Does he spend the PE lessons with the rest of his class?
    b Where does he spend playtimes?
3 Are his parents involved in your programme for him?
    a Have you met his parents and discussed their problems?
    b Can his parents talk to you?

   c   Are they able to visit you easily?

   d   Are the parents formally invited to discuss their child's programme with you?

4 How does he get on with the other children?

   a   Is he 'out on a limb'?

   b   Is he laughed at?

   c   Can he talk about his handicap?

   d   Does he take advantage of the good nature of his peers?

As regards question 1, access may prove to be a major problem. The toilets may not be large enough to accommodate a wheelchair. There may be no handrails at the toilet and sinks to help the child on sticks. Would it be possible to make the necessary alterations?

With reference to the other points in this section, it is very difficult not to make a special case out of the handicapped child in a class. However this is doing the child a grave injustice, for it only succeeds in making him appear very different in the eyes of his peers. Moreover it can have the damaging effect of giving the child himself a very poor self image. To illustrate our point, one handicapped child known to us had a squad of his classmates assigned to the task of carrying him upstairs. These boys, eventually regarded as lackeys by the handicapped lad, must have hated being treated as servants. It is sad to reflect on the opinion they may well have had of all handicapped persons, as a result of this one experience.

To help one another is, of course, part of our day to day lives, but would it not have been more dignified for that particular boy to have been enabled to get around in his wheelchair, with the same independence his classmates enjoyed? Would it not have been kinder to all concerned to have planned his timetable so that whenever possible he had his lessons on the ground floor?

For a physically handicapped child to succeed in the normal school it is vital for the school to liaise closely with the child's medical consultants, his parents, his physiotherapist and his occupational therapist. In fact thorough assessments by an informed psychologist, a medical consultant and a physiotherapist are essential to give the school a base line on which to build a relevant and practical educational programme. Then the school as a whole must form short and long term goals for the child. To achieve this it is important that *all* the staff involved with the child sit down together – ideally with the specialists, or failing that with their reports – and plan a realistic programme. Then the physically handicapped child can be included in all lessons, especially the PE and games lessons.

These in particular do, however, require a lot of thought. A circuit such as the one described in Chapter Four could well be part of the school's PE curriculum. As will be seen from the chapter on games, there are many that are suitable, possibly with small adaptations, for the handicapped child to join in with his class mates. The handicapped child may be able to referee. Is this not a better alternative to spending the games lesson in the library?

Finally, it is always worth considering who is actually benefiting from your 'help' – you or the child? Are you providing the best possible means for the handicapped child in your class to enjoy an independent life?

3   The Pre-School Child

What does one do when told that one's child is handicapped? The initial shock is obviously very great and at the beginning one can only rely on the care and understanding of the medical staff involved and on the support of one's family.

Once the parents have come to terms with the situation, it is natural for them to want to do the best for their child. In many areas of Britain they are given help, advice and guidance, usually via the hospital in which the child was first seen.

In addition, parents may find it helpful and reassuring to contact the specific group with experience of their child's particular handicap – for example the Spastics Society, the Association for Spina Bifida and Hydrocephalus, the Muscular Dystrophy Group of Great Britain, etc. – the addresses of which will be found at the end of the book.

Useful books of general reference are usually available from occupational therapy departments. In some hospitals an 'aids centre' has a good supply of the latest equipment, books and ideas.

Another source of reference is the local school for physically handicapped children. The schools are usually happy to advise on the best reference source or self help groups in the area.

Opportunity groups are also being set up, either by local community groups or by local handicap groups employed by the Health Service or Council. These groups usually involve peripatetic agencies such as social workers, physiotherapists and occupational therapists whose advice and treatment skills may be used. The groups involve the handicapped child's brothers and sisters within the age group. The mother, for her part, can either join in the group's activities or leave her child there, while she has time to herself. Or she can opt to join the group for some of the time. The local hospital or school can usually put parents in touch with the nearest group.

The family doctor will probably be an excellent source of

information, too, and very willing to help if asked. He may also have notices and information in the surgery.

However, as with all children, in the final analysis everything comes back to the parents, on whose support and guidance every child greatly depends, especially in his early years. But as the parents of a physically handicapped child may lack confidence, usually because they know few or no other similar handicapped children on whom to base their approach, we feel it may be helpful to suggest a few guidelines.

It is natural to base one's expectations of one's child on the achievements of previous children or of children one knows, but one may then become terribly frustrated because one's handicapped child is not progressing as one feels he should. If the parent gives up, this sense of failure transfers to the child.

It is therefore most important to have realistic expectations for one's child. If one expects nothing, the child will do nothing. Conversely, if one expects too much, one will end up completely frustrated and probably again achieve nothing. The essential approach is to find out what one can realistically expect of one's child and then to encourage him to be as independent as possible within his limitations. We realise that this is easier said than done, for the patience and time needed may sap the energy of even the most determined parent.

It is impossible to generalise about the way one should cope with a handicapped child, for each one is different, with different parents. However, it is important that the child should remain as supple as possible and should be given every possible opportunity for experience. For this the parent will need the help of a physiotherapist who can advise on possible aids and demonstrate the kind of exercises and stretchings necessary to stimulate the child. He can also demonstrate to the parent how to position the child so that he can enjoy normal developmental experiences. For example, in order to play with sand or water, the child may need to be 'propped' in a certain way. The physiotherapist can show the parent how this may comfortably and safely be achieved.

The staff of the local special school will only be too pleased to suggest suitable constructive play material and to give advice on basic independence skills. The earlier the child begins to learn these, the better. It is very much more difficult to learn to cope with an appliance at the age of 12 when one has always totally relied on someone else to do it, than gradually to learn the process from the earliest possible age. Moreover, unless a handicapped child begins to learn from an early age that his body is *his* responsibility, he can grow up to think that his body is somebody else's chore and nothing to do with him – an attitude which ultimately does nothing for his self respect and, to use the present day jargon, gives him a poor self image.

Perhaps, as a parent, you might sit down with your child and a pile of coloured bricks. You say to him, 'Build a tower from those red bricks on the table' – an apparently simple task that most young toddlers enjoy. You then find that your child cannot do as you ask. However, if you analyse what you have asked him to do, the seemingly simple instruction acquires a variety of implications and a wealth of assumed skills which an able-bodied child has absorbed, unobserved by anyone, simply because he can explore his environment unaided. For example, an able-bodied child will toddle off into the garden and by chance bend down and play with the soil. He will find, again most likely by chance, that there is a big difference between wet and dry soil. When it is dry, the child can put it into his wheelbarrow and make a pile of it. When it is wet, it is all sticky and squidgy, and so on. But a handicapped child, who is unable to move under his own steam, will not even discover the soil unless someone takes him to it and puts him within its reach. This is perhaps the overriding problem for a handicapped child. His world is so small and his natural experiences so limited unless someone purposely introduces him to all those things which he cannot come across naturally. An able-bodied child will happen on a mirror and discover a wealth of new experiences simply by looking into it. Someone will have to bring a mirror to a handicapped child and prop it so that he can look into it.

So, to return to the tower of red bricks. What are we assuming? Why cannot the child complete the task?

a   What position is the child in to perform the task? Can he climb from the floor to the chair to reach the bricks? Can he pull himself to a standing position to be able to reach the table from the floor? Is he concentrating so hard on keeping his balance that he cannot put his mind to picking up the bricks?

b Does he understand that by 'build' you mean 'place one on top of the other'?

c Does he comprehend 'on the table' and therefore know where to look?

d Does he know his colours? Can he differentiate between one colour and another and therefore be able to choose the right bricks?

e Is he able to grasp the brick in one or both hands?

f Is his hand control steady enough to allow him to place one brick on top of the other without knocking the tower down?

Even the simplest of tasks become very complex when broken down in this way. Moreover, it takes quite a lot of experience to be able to break down and reduce a task to its simplest form; and then to be able to build on it until one achieves the original task set. This is where those who work with handicapped children can often help the anxious parent.

How can the parents best help their handicapped child to develop, within the home environment? Again it is impossible to generalise, for every family situation is different. If in doubt, the best thing the parents can do is ask their doctor for a domiciliary visit by an occupational therapist, physiotherapist or teacher who can then assess the situation and make suggestions.

There are two extremes in family attitudes – the deprived on the one hand, the over-protected on the other. Neither is desirable for any child. Somewhere between the two is the ideal situation where a child can go out and explore his environment (within reason), bruise his shin, make a decision, get dirty, be part of a group. All parents have the responsibility of deciding what is 'reasonable freedom' in their particular situation with their particular child. They can only do what they believe to be right and have confidence in their decision. The same parent may find he or she is criticised by one person for giving too much freedom and by another for over-protecting!

For the parents of a physically handicapped child, the problem is more difficult because it is more time consuming and more demanding; because initially they have to think ahead for their child and must often set up a situation to enable their child to have the experience. For example, the able-bodied child will jump on a chair to look into a mirror; the mirror will have to be purposely placed for a physically handicapped child.

Nonetheless, within the daily family routine the parents should try to work out when they can give time to their child to develop his motor skills in as natural a way as possible.

Three possible situations are:
a Dressing
b Feeding
c Bathing

a *Dressing*

It is important to remember that you must not expect too much, and to praise any achievement of your child, however small. This obviously involves knowing your child and having the confidence to 'have a go'. A few guidelines which may prove helpful are:

(i) It is easier to undress than dress, so help your child to succeed in taking his clothes off before you expect him to put them on.

(ii) Your child must be in a well supported, comfortable position. Initially this may be lying on his side or on his tummy if the child cannot sit, or sitting in a bean bag chair or supported with pillows. If you cannot find a comfortable position get professional help from an occupational therapist or physiotherapist.

(iii) Use suitable clothes, with the minimum of fiddly fastenings: for example, elasticated trousers are more easily taken off than buttoned ones; velcro fastenings are easier than hooks and eyes; envelope necks can be removed with greater ease than fastened necks; two-piece outfits are easier than all-in-one suits.

b *Feeding*

(i) Find the right position for your child. He must be really well supported so that, to begin with, he can concentrate totally on hand control. When he has mastered that, balance can be worked on.

(ii) Use suitable implements – for example, non-slip mats,

thick handled spoons, 'bent' spoons. These can be seen at the Occupational Therapy Aids Centre.

(iii)   Give the child enough time and encouragement.

(iv)   Try to get the child to feed with the rest of the family. Only give him his fair share of your attention and time.

c   *Bathing*

This is an ideal opportunity for play and for exploring the environment – for example, splashing, grasping toys, pouring from one container into the bath or into another container, blowing bubbles, getting water onto the face, deciding which toy to play with. A mirror placed where the child can see himself can be a great source of fun. Use a rubber mat if necessary. Talk to your child. Play with him, for your play will stimulate his.

4 The Special School Child – the Team Approach

HOW THE CIRCUIT WORKS

Once the child begins school, he is in almost daily contact with teachers, medical staff, occupational therapists and physiotherapists, all of whom should be working together to develop his body and mind.

The idea of the Cedar School circuit gradually evolved from the realisation of the fact that, within a very short school day, not only were the children expected to be 'educated' in the broadest sense, but they were expected to practise their independence skills and perform the other tasks allotted to them by the physiotherapist, the occupational therapist and medical staff. Thus in the course of one day, a child might easily be taken out of class on at least three separate occasions – not to mention demands on his time made by speech therapists, psychologists, hospital and doctors' visits.

A way to prevent this and to provide the children with motivation and purpose for some of their more boring physical tasks began to evolve after much discussion.

It was realised very early on that the team approach was vital. The interaction of ideas, among a group of specialists striving towards a common objective, produces results in much the same way as horses pulling together to draw a cart. Not a lot of progress is made if the horses each pull in a different direction!

Members of the Cedar School team include the PE teacher, the physiotherapist, the occupational therapist, the nurse, care staff and voluntary helpers. Each team member has his part to play in the circuit.

1 The Role of the PE Teacher

He is generally in charge of the whole session. It is up to him to organise a programme in such a way that each individual child realises his full physical potential. If the teacher succeeds in this, the children will be fit and will enjoy and understand the rules of a game, whether it be a game of table tennis or wheelchair football. They will learn to play *together*, to lose in the right spirit, to enjoy themselves. Moreover they will acquire interests which hopefully will be developed later.

2 The Role of the Physiotherapist

Together with the PE teacher, the physiotherapist plans the circuit to incorporate necessary physical exercises. Her ultimate aim is the physical independence of each child. She strives for physical well being and fitness, for maintenance, acquisition and improvement of muscle strength and tone which will enable the child to function as effectively as possible, within the limits of his physical handicap. For example, she teaches him to manoeuvre himself, his wheelchair, his sticks and his calipers.

She advises on the safety of movement and how a particular child can safely complete a particular task. For example, to get from the floor to a wheelchair, a child may get up forwards, backwards, sideways from another chair, reverse up steps, stand, pull into the chair with a helper standing behind, need one aid to lift him or two people to lift him.

She advises members of the team in the event of the latter suggesting an activity which could be harmful to the child. For example, sliding along the floor for a spina bifida child may cause friction burns because such children have altered sensation.

The physiotherapist can also use this opportunity to check each child's 'equipment' – wheelchair, calipers and boots – whilst still leaving the responsibility for them to the child.

She will watch the children go round the circuit and study the changes in their ability. For example, she will initially see how much aid is necessary for a child to get from the floor to the chair and she will judge when it can be decreased.

If a child seems to be having difficulty in a particular area it is up to her to find out if there is a specific problem. For instance, she monitors the degree of scoliosis in the child with spina bifida; she watches to see if the child has outgrown his calipers or is about to do so; she judges whether a child is realising his maximum potential. All these activities are part of the physiotherapist's brief. For a physiotherapist with an interest in sport, what better way is there to combine her brief and her interest?

3 The Role of the Occupational Therapist

She has full responsibility for the dressing and undressing of the children before and after the games session. She teaches a vital life skill but in a situation *with a purpose*. What can be more soul destroying than undressing for no reason? The occupational therapist will understand how to overcome the problems of dressing and can therefore break them down into a series of easy steps.

4 The Role of the Nurse

As there is a large number of children with urinary diversions, there is usually a nurse present whose role is to teach the care and use of appliances. Since the child is changing for games, it is an ideal opportunity for the nurse to supervise the emptying and changing of appliances as necessary. Depending on the level of ability attained by the child, the nurse will give more or less help. Obviously, to make the child spend the whole of the games session changing his bag defeats the purpose of the exercise! In a school where the day is longer and facilities permit, it should be possible for the children to shower after games and thus a self care programme may be practically introduced.

5 Care Staff

These are vital members of the team. Many are NNEB or similarly trained. They are invaluable in helping to train in dressing and toileting and in helping to lift.

6 Voluntary Helpers

They are essential. PE students from the local college and school leavers are often keen to help.

The Team as a Whole

If the team is to be effective, it is vital that each member understands and appreciates the role of the others in the team. This will mean that each must be prepared to 'step back' and let another team member take the lead in certain circumstances, however frustrating. For example, Rupert has to leave the session early because the occupational therapist is at a crucial stage in his dressing programme and needs the extra time. It is a good idea for the team members to meet as a group and discuss the individual children. In this way priorities can be decided upon, and all can be 'pulling in the same direction'. As with any group of people working together, the team approach works if the individuals get on well together as people. Their enthusiasm and belief in what they are doing will generate an atmosphere of enjoyment which will perpetrate new ideas. The enthusiasm of the team will transfer to the children who will therefore perform well and in turn give added incentive to the team.

THE CIRCUIT
The circuit is set up in a hall, which in the Cedar School is also used as dining room/assembly hall and classroom as well as being used as the games hall.

The initial group to use the circuit consisted of, on average, twenty children at each session, with a variety of physical handicap. There were 11 children with spina bifida, five with cerebral palsy, one with muscular dystrophy, one haemophiliac and two with connective tissue disorders.

The largest group was therefore the spina bifida and of the 11 children in this group, three were ambulant and the remainder in wheelchairs. Of the cerebral palsy children, all five were ambulant, one using a frame initially, one using sticks all the time and another who used sticks for the first few sessions. The haemophiliac was ambulant, except when he had a leg bleed at which times he would be confined to a wheelchair. The muscular dystrophy was a Duchenne boy in an electric wheelchair. The final two children had an undiagnosed connective tissue disorder and were both in wheelchairs.

When setting out the circuit, it is advisable to clear away as much unused furniture as possible from the area to be used. As the children who use the circuit often find concentration a real problem, the fewer distractions the better.

The circuit consists of ten exercises determined by the physical education teacher and the physiotherapist. They are set out in a circular pattern so that the children progress, in pairs, round the circuit from one exercise to the next until they have completed all ten. Each exercise is performed for a minute's duration and each child counts for himself and remembers how many times he performs the exercise. Both ambulant and wheelchair children are equally able to do each exercise. Specific modifications become obvious as one reads the section. To make the direction of flow doubly clear, each exercise is clearly labelled with a large number. In addition, a large clear chart of the circuit is well placed for easy reference by the participants. Our pilot group, which consisted of seniors, was very soon able to discard these props, but successive groups of younger children did not find it quite so easy to manage without them. Thus the diagrams and numbers should always be clearly visible. The chart should be large and as near a diagrammatic representation of the circuit as possible. A child who finds it difficult to follow a sequence may need much skilled help to overcome his problem. Since our pilot group could all count, numbering the activities proved an adequate guide for them. However, with a non-counting group, perhaps a different system could be devised. For example, large arrows could be taped to the floor, or a system of coloured dots, increasing or decreasing in size, could be placed around the circuit.

These systems, including the numbers, may also encourage counting and sequencing. It may be necessary to draw a diagram of each exercise on the number, if the wall chart is not easily accessible to every participant in the circuit. However, this should only be a temporary aid or the 'circuit' idea may become a set of disjointed exercises to many children, rather than an integral whole. And thus the whole point of the circuit idea will be lost.

A typical chart may therefore look something like the one opposite. The use of bright colours will make it easier to understand.

Perceptually this is as easy as is possible for the greater number of our children.

As can be seen from the chart, the floor exercises are grouped together, so that the child gets onto the floor at least once during the session.

The sequence of the circuit can be changed, according to the ability of the children involved. For example, if you have a large number of children who need practice in getting in and out of wheelchairs, the activities can be placed in such a way

1. FORMS

10. RAMP

2. BALL ROUND BODY

9. SLALOM RUN

3. PRESS UPS

8. BASKETBALL

4. SIT UPS

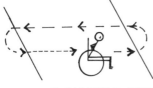

7. SHUTTLE RUN

5. PUSH UPS

6. SPRINGS

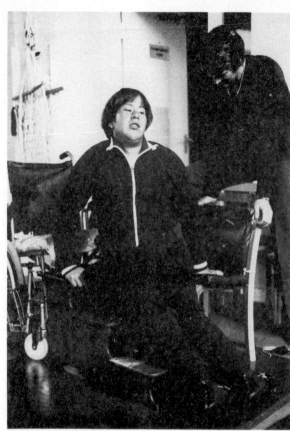

Transferring from the floor to a wheelchair.

Rolling along the floor.

that the children have to do this more often. If, as in our case, moving from the wheelchair was a major problem, the circuit would be arranged so as to make this necessary only once.

However, it is necessary for the participants to move along the floor. Therefore we usually leave a gap of several metres between the last two floor exercises, to accommodate this. This is an ideal opportunity for the physiotherapist to observe the children. For example:

1   The cerebral palsy child may choose to crawl over the distance. Is he crawling reciprocally?

2   The spina bifida child moves backwards. He may at first drag his lower limbs and seat, exposing them to sores. It would therefore be much safer for him to sit with his legs straight and lift his bottom back on his arms. This way, the only danger area is the heel.

3   The child with muscular dystrophy who is unable to move very far at all may be able to roll across the distance. This will give him a great feeling of independence.

4   The child with the connective tissue disorder may be able to sit in the long sitting position and use whatever leg power he has, in conjunction with an arm lift to go across backwards. This is also very useful for giving the legs a good stretch, if performed well.

5   The spina bifida child who walks infrequently but usually stands for periods during the day, may use this opportunity to walk a short distance. A helper is usually vital to the success of this operation.

6   The very heavily handicapped cerebral palsy child may well be able to develop his own means of locomotion on the floor here. We have one such child who developed a style of amphibian creep. His sense of achievement was indescribable.

When setting up the circuit it is important that any equipment that may be required is present at the relevant section and thus available to the child. We have certain children for example who are unable to long-sit on the floor due to inflexibility at the hips. They may therefore need special chairs for the more static floor work, which should be placed at the relevant exercises beforehand. The individuals can eventually be made responsible for their own special equipment, although initially this may prove an excessive demand. With our pilot group, one term was all that was necessary for them actually to be setting up the whole circuit for themselves. They were keen to take on the responsibility and could eventually set it up more quickly than the staff!

Dependent on the number of children going round the circuit, enough apparatus must be placed to accommodate them. So if children are going round in pairs, there must be two forms, two balls, two springs, etc. If the children are going round in threes, then three of each piece of apparatus are necessary.

The apparatus should be regularly checked, especially any wooden apparatus, as many of the spina bifida children have no, or altered sensation in their lower limbs. It may be with an older group that the 'maintenance' is a task for the children on a rota basis. This will make them aware of the pitfalls and problems of wooden equipment. It will also encourage them to take care of themselves. However, it should not be a job left solely to the children at any stage, but supervised by a member of the team.

THE ACTIVITIES OF THE CIRCUIT

1 Forms

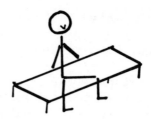

For this exercise, the participant transfers from the wheelchair to the form. Having made the move, the exercise is to progress along the form sideways, by lifting the bottom and then the legs. Each time the child travels along the bench a point is scored.

This exercise has obvious advantages for the wheelchair user, as transfers are an integral part of wheelchair life. Initially it may have to be done in stages; it may be necessary at first to decrease the height required to transfer if the form is very low. This can be done by putting a stool of intermediate height

Forms – sideways transfer.

between the wheelchair and the form. Alternatively a sliding board may be used. (This is a well varnished wooden board. The child bridges the gap between the chair and the form by moving along the board. It is available from most occupational therapy departments or a friendly woodwork teacher!)

Transferring from the wheelchair to the form also tests wheelchair abilities. Can the child get the arm out of his chair? Can he manoeuvre his chair to the best position by the form? Can he swing out his footrests – and so on?

If a particular child is unable to do the exercise, one must work out the reason for his lack of success. Are his arms strong enough to lift his body across? Can he manage his own legs? Does he understand what he has to do? Would he be able to transfer forwards? Are the wheelchair arms rusty? Is the perception of the space between the chair and the form too terrifying to attempt?

For the ambulant child with co-ordination problems – for example, the cerebral palsies – to put both hands to the form, with his feet flat on the floor at the same time as lifting his bottom, can become a very involved task.

One of the major aims of this exercise is to improve balance. For without a sense of balance it is impossible to transfer from a wheelchair. Moreover, as many children suffer from a lack of balance and are unaware of the position of their body in space, it is essential to have someone standing behind each child to prevent him from falling and to give him the confidence to do the exercise.

Scoring: It must be emphasised that the *whole* of the bench must be used for a point to be scored.

Other ideas, based on the forms, are:

    a   To walk along the form.

    b   To lie horizontally on the form and pull the whole body along it.

    c   To do bunny hops along the form – either with both hands and feet on the form, or with the hands on the form while hopping over the form from one side to the other.

2 Pass Ball round Body

Use as large a ball as possible. Sit upright with the legs together and stretched out straight as far as is possible within the restrictions of the handicap. The ball must pass around the back and in front of the feet.

The skills developed in this exercise are:

    (i)   Hand, eye co-ordination. Those children with perceptual problems find this exercise very difficult, especially when the ball goes around behind them!

    (ii)   The hamstring muscles get a good stretch.

    (iii) The balance and co-ordination required to sit with the legs straight prove quite a challenge to all!

The exercise can be made more difficult by using a progressively smaller ball.

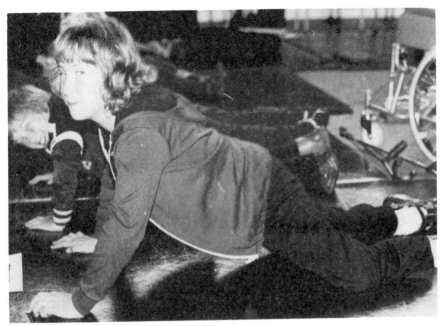

Press-ups.

Scoring: A point is scored for every completed circle round the body.

3 Press-Ups

As far as possible, lie flat on the tummy, with the palms of the hands flat on the floor, directly underneath the shoulders. Keep the body rigid. Ideally there should be no bending at the tummy. The body should be like a log, but it must be remembered that the child with spina bifida will be unable to push up with his legs as struts, and a very heavily handicapped cerebral palsy may only be able to lift his head to start with.

This exercise will develop arm strength. Bilateral exercise of this kind will help to prevent scoliosis.

Scoring: One point is scored every time the body is off the ground.

4   Sit-Ups

Lie on the back with the hands either crossed over the chest (harder!) or lying on top of thighs (but not holding on to the tracksuit!). Tighten the tummy muscles then start to sit up – ideally until the head is about 30 cms (12″) off the ground. Then lie back and relax the abdominal muscles. Repeat. Bear in mind that to begin with most children will sit right up. Allow this. Some may hold on to their trousers or sit up by a rotary movement with the help of one arm. Allow this provided that the child uses both sides alternately. If you find that the children are not able to succeed at all then begin by lifting a light beach ball from the back of the head towards the feet.

Later incorporate raising the head and then the shoulders. Finally, dispose of the ball.

This exercise will strengthen the abdominal muscles. Care must be taken that the child who sits up to one side, uses both his sides – to prevent scoliosis.

Scoring: One point is scored each time the head leaves the ground.

5   Push-Ups

Sit on the floor with the legs straight out in front and the knuckles (or palms of the hands) on the floor in line with the hips. Lift the bottom up by pushing on the hands. Do not shrug the shoulders. Repeat.

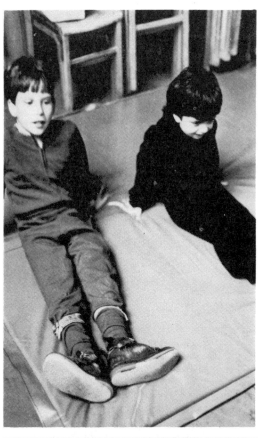

Push-ups.

Springs.

This exercise was introduced with the wheelchair child in mind. He must be able to raise his bottom from the chair or floor to prevent pressure sores. Ideally anyone in a wheelchair should do this about five times in an hour, as a matter of course. Those of us with sensation are constantly changing position, as we get uncomfortable. It is important to remember that not all children in wheelchairs can feel. For the cerebral palsy child this exercise encourages balance and co-ordination. In the early stages he will need a lot of encouragement because he finds it extremely difficult to get it all together.

Scoring: One point every time the bottom leaves the ground.

6   Springs

Attach a pair of springs of equal poundage to the wall-bars. With his back to the wall-bars, the child grasps the handles, one in each hand, and pulls, maintaining a stationary position with his trunk. The springs can be pulled, (a) over the shoulder, or (b) under the arm.

Alternatively the child can face the wall-bars and pull. It is important to make sure, (a) that the brakes of the wheelchair are on, (b) that any ordinary chair used is flush with the wall-bars to prevent the chair tipping during the exercise and (c) that the child controls the recoil of the spring as well as pulling it out.

This exercise can be done with equal ease by the child in a wheelchair and the ambulant child. The children who sit to do the exercise (either in a wheelchair or on a chair) should ensure that their feet are firmly on the floor or footrests with a 90° angle of flexion at the hips, knees and ankles. They should sit well back in the chair so that they are as well balanced as possible. They can thus concentrate on the exercise, rather than on sitting still. Obviously the springs must be of equal power to ensure an equal pull, enabling the child to keep his back straight.

If the child seems unable to pull the springs without moving the trunk, try a decrease in the power of the springs. If that fails, pass two strings over a wall-bar (like two pulleys) and tie bean bags or skittles to the other ends. Let the child pull the objects up and down in the manner previously described. Bilateral activity must be encouraged at all times. For example, in the spina bifida child who has a tendency to curvature of the spine (scoliosis), unilateral activity will exacerbate this problem. With the cerebral palsy child, imbalance is a great problem. Bilateral activity wherever possible encourages muscle balance. This would also apply to the children with muscular problems – dystrophy and atrophy.

Scoring: One point every time the springs are fully extended.

7 Shuttle Run

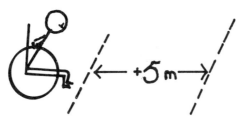

Mark out two lines, at least 5 m apart. The child starts behind one of the lines and has to propel himself as fast as possible to the other line. Wheelchair users must go completely over the line. Children who can walk and bend should touch the ground beyond the line, before turning. This is an exercise which combines speed and manoeuvrability. It is a very interesting exercise perceptually, since the child has to determine the position of the lines and then to accomplish a 180° turn, with the minimum of wasted effort. Turning on the spot in a wheelchair, involving a forwards movement with one hand, and a backwards movement with the other, can for some very perceptually handicapped children prove to be an extremely complicated task. These children will prefer to manoeuvre round in a large arc, involving only the forward movement of their chair.

Instead of   they will

This creates the additional problem, increased in proportion to the arc made, of avoiding a crash with the other participants in the exercise.

This exercise can be made more difficult by moving backwards, requiring a great deal of skill as well as the ability to look behind. We have found that many children ignore the fact that someone or even something may be behind them, when they want to reverse! The children should be well practised at reversing before being allowed to try the reverse shuttle in their pairs!

Stamina is greatly improved by the shuttle run. Most children find themselves far less breathless – after a few weeks' practice!

Needless to say the cardiac children and the haemophiliacs should be carefully watched and encouraged to perform at a steady jogging pace. A dystrophy child can complete this exercise in his wheelchair.

Scoring: One point for going across the space and one point for going back.

8 Basketball Bounce

Using a basket ball, the child aims to bounce it continuously with one hand. The children find this exercise one of the most complicated in the circuit. They are required to sit or stand, if possible unsupported, and bounce the basket ball with either hand. This exercise requires careful thought if the child is to complete it satisfactorily, for it is quite an advanced skill to bounce a ball in this way. If a child is unable to do this exercise successfully, it may be best to reduce the skill to its basics:

1   Ask the helper to throw and catch the ball with the child, using a large air-filled ball.
2   Throw the ball against a wall and catch it.
3   Move progressively farther away from the wall.

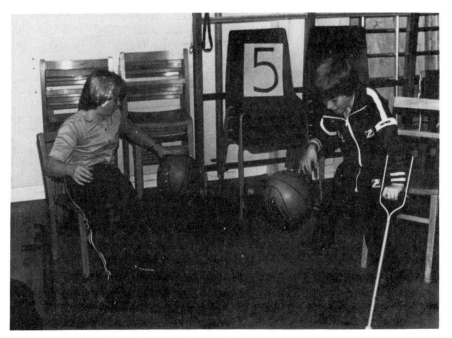

Basketball bounce.

The beginnings
of basketball.

4 Bounce and catch the ball, with both hands in front, on a large raised area – a low table will do if nothing else is to hand.
5 Put the table to the side of the child.
6 Lower the table until the child is bouncing the ball and catching it on the floor.
7 Progress to using only one hand.

There are several points to consider in the event of problems. Can the child in the wheelchair pick up the ball, should he drop it? (See Skills Circuit Exercise One, p 66.) Can he reach the ball on the floor, or should he remove the arm from his wheelchair? If he removes the arm from his wheelchair to lean out, does he need to wear a belt to help him maintain his balance? Finally, if he is not happy leaning out, is it because he is afraid of falling due to a lack of balance, or has he got perceptual problems as regards the anticipation of the space between himself and the floor?

As for the ambulant child who has difficulty in doing this exercise, can he balance adequately to perform the task? Would he be able to balance if he were supported on one side (diagram a)? Would he perform better if he were in a high kneeling position (diagram b), in a cross-legged position (diagram c) or side sitting position (diagram d)?

a   b   c   d

With the muscular dystrophy children, a large beach ball often permits them to perform this exercise competently.
Scoring: A point is scored each time the ball hits the hand.

9 Slalom Run

Place three or four skittles in a straight line, approximately 2 m apart. The child has to weave in and out of the skittles, with a turn at the end before the return run.

Reduce the distance between the skittles as the children become more competent, until the skittles are 70–80 cm apart which is the national competitive wheelchair standard in this event. At first this exercise is performed going forward; eventually, it can be made more difficult by the children going backwards. As with the shuttle run, it must be established that the child is perceptually aware of the task. The child may find it a real challenge when asked to go backwards. The ambulant child can also go backwards – even those with a rollator – with practice!

This exercise aims to improve balance, co-ordination and manoeuvrability.

Scoring: One point each time the child turns.

10 Ramps and Steps

For the final exercise in the circuit a certain amount of furniture is required, and a friendly carpenter may be willing to build a ramp, a platform and a short stairway (for specifications see page 56).

The ramp consists of a kerb platform (see diagram p 56) and a slalom ramp (see diagram p 56) for wheelchair users and some walkers. Steps are used by the more able walkers and a bench by the most able walkers. Thus each child uses the piece of equipment that best suits his need.

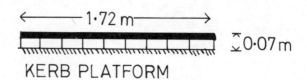

KERB PLATFORM

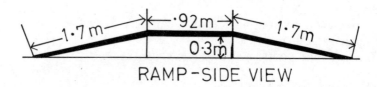

RAMP-SIDE VIEW

RAMP-TOP VIEW

a *Ramp*

The ramp is normally used by the wheelchair participant. Some children have a lot of problems with this piece of equipment. Points to be considered when doing this exercise are:

(i)   To be off the ground in a wheelchair is initially a very frightening experience.

(ii)   Some of the children have difficulty in judging their position in relation to the edge of the ramp. It is therefore essential for a helper to guide the wheelchair – from behind when going up the slope, and from in front when going down the slope.

(iii)   Many children are afraid of falling out of the wheelchair on the downward slope, therefore they must be well strapped in.

(iv)   Ensure that the participants are aware of just how to negotiate the slope. That is they must, (a) lean forward as they go up, (b) always keep a steady pressure on the wheels, (c) lean slightly backwards when going down and (d) use the hands to act as brakes on the wheels.

To complete this exercise successfully, the participant must be able to manoeuvre the wheelchair within fairly narrow limits, have enough strength in the upper trunk to enable him to get the wheelchair up the slope and have fairly good balance.

One of our older children was eventually able to go up the ramp on his rear wheels, remain so while he executed a 360° turn and then proceed down the ramp again, still on his rear wheels. For a fairly high lesion spina bifida boy, this was no small feat.

Apart from the wheelchair group:

(i)   Children on rollators should be able to manage a slight slope.

(ii)   Those who are in calipers with a pelvic band and who jump, with the help of a rollator, may find it easier to go down ramps backwards, unless they are very gradual, as the rollators have a tendency to tip forwards.

(iii)   Some of our less ambulant children who have muscular problems also find ramps easier to manage than stairs, if given practice.

Scoring: One point each time the child goes over the ramp.

 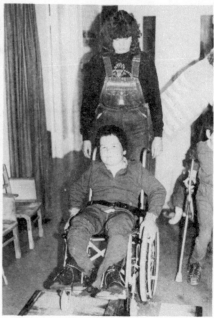

Ramp.   Kerb platform.

b *Kerb Platform*
This is a most useful piece of equipment for beginning the rudiments of 'kerb drill'. It can therefore be used by both walkers and wheelchair users.

(i) The wheelchair users must learn to 'flick' the front wheels of their chairs, to get them up onto the kerb platform. This is achieved by leaning back and at the same time giving a sharp forwards push on the wheel which forces the front wheels up and slightly forwards on to the kerb. Once the front castors are on the platform, the trunk is inclined forwards and the back wheels can then be pushed forwards.
Once the wheelchair is on top of the platform the chair is turned 180° on the spot (much manoeuvring skill is necessary to accomplish this). Then the descent from the kerb must be backwards. The child must at this point lean forwards to prevent the wheelchair from tipping backwards.
(ii) The walkers – even those who use rollators – can also use this apparatus as the beginnings of stair or kerb drill.

Children who use rollators must be able to take their weight on to their feet and tip one of the front wheels of the rollator up onto the platform. They then repeat the procedure for the other wheel, push the rollator on to the platform and finally step onto the platform themselves. We tend to teach the children with rollators to come down backwards. However, some children with a reciprocal gait can complete the manoeuvre forwards without tipping the rollator.

Scoring: One point for each trip across the platform.

c *Stairs and Hand Rail*
For the more ambulant children the stairs are used for the performance of step-ups. Starting with the feet on the ground, the participant steps onto the first step and then steps back down again. Some children who have pelvic band or above knee calipers can only perform this exercise double legged, ie they jump.

Scoring: One point each time the child steps up.

d *Benches*
For the most ambulant, the bench is used for step-ups. The child repeatedly steps up onto the bench and back down again.

Scoring: One point for each step up.

The Placing of Staff for the Circuit
The placing of staff available to help with the running of the circuit is a matter for the team to discuss and decide upon. It is usually necessary for a member of staff to be at Exercises 1 (forms) and 10 (ramp – platform – steps), because there is difficult apparatus in use here and if the children are unskilled, there is a risk of falling. If one is working with a group of children who have difficulty in getting to and from the floor (either from chair, rollator or sticks) it is necessary for a trained team member to be present at each exercise where this occurs. With a skilled group of children, however, the minimum of staff supervision is necessary. Even the timing can be done by a Duchenne boy from his electric wheelchair.

It should always be possible for the staff to join in on the circuit with the children. This not only serves to keep the staff fit but greatly adds to the motivation and enjoyment of the children. There is nothing like setting a good example!

Scoring
Sometimes helpers are needed for counting and to run spot checks.

The circuit is timed for a minute on each exercise. Between each exercise, there is a minute or a minute and a half's rest. To begin with, the gap between each exercise may have to be longer with an unskilled group, to accommodate their various problems with manoeuvring and generally sorting themselves out. In our pilot group the scores were kept by a Duchenne boy in an electric wheelchair, who compiled the charts for the group and kept each individual's score for each exercise.

A typical chart for 8th November may be:

	Forms	Balls	Press-ups	Sit-ups	Push-ups	Springs	Shuttle	Basket	Slalom	Ramp	Total 1st Nov.	Total 8th Nov.
Fred B.	1	6	10	20	30	10	6	40	3	3	120	129
John S.	2	9	9	16	35	11	5	50	1	2	119	140
Sara P.	3	7	11	15	40	15	8	52	5	4	156	160

Each child is required to count and to remember his own score. During the rest period between each exercise, the scorer calls out each child's name and records his score.

The beauty of this system is that each child is in competition, but only with himself. We have introduced a medal system so that the child who makes the most progress in the course of one month is awarded the gold medal for the following month. With this system, it is very often not the most able child who makes the most progress. In fact one of our most heavily handicapped children made the gold medal position in our first month. The reward is for individual effort rather than natural ability. The timer controls both the timing of the session and the scoring. This gives him a feeling of responsibility and power! Depending on the group of children doing the circuit, it may be a good idea for them to take turns at this job. For example, in one of our groups there were two Duchenne boys who took turns at being the timer.

Self scoring encourages self discipline and honesty. Anyone

who is short sighted enough to add unearned points to his score, gives himself a great problem the following week!!

The Benefits gained from the Circuit

1 *Enjoyment and fun* The children enjoy doing the circuit and get a lot of fun from it.

2 *Physical Fitness* If you are still not convinced of the value of the circuit in building up physical fitness, it is interesting to see the results of vitalagraph readings, taken at the beginning of the term, compared with those taken on the same children at the end of term. Similarly, resting heart rates taken at the beginning of the term differ dramatically from those taken at the end of the term.

3 *Independence* The children have to think for themselves and be responsible for their own management. A simple instruction like 'two of you to each piece of apparatus' may initially cause utter confusion among a group of children who are used to having others think for them and sometimes even talk for them. As far as is possible, the children dress themselves. As the responsibility is on them, they learn to put their clothes on properly, to avoid being laughed at. Each new achievement is given praise and encouragement. In this way the children develop a good self image and gain in confidence.

4 *Social Awareness* The children are encouraged by the circuit to get along in a group.

5 *The Development of Perceptual Skills* Damage to parts of the cerebrum results in 'perceptual problems'. These are:

a Body awareness. A handicapped child may not be aware of all the body's parts or that some are larger than others, or that many parts make up the whole. He may therefore find it difficult to relate one part of his body to another.

b The use of space. Not only are some handicapped children unaware of where parts of their body are, but they also have difficulty in relating their body to those of other people or to the things around them. They may find it equally difficult to select a given item from a group of items. This could make team games extremely difficult for them!

If a child has perceptual problems, even the simplest task may become very complicated for him. For example, how can he 'get into a line' for a team game if he has no concept of 'one behind the other'? An obstacle course can be an extremely difficult task for the child who cannot perceive 'over', 'under', 'through', and so on. The circuit helps the children to meet and to overcome some of their perceptual problems.

6   *The Development of Gross and Fine Motor Skills*   The gross motor skills are those which involve the whole body either as a single unit (as in press-ups, sit-ups) or as part of a group (as in the shuttle run where it is important not to crash into the others). The fine motor skills are those which require a greater degree of manual dexterity, such as doing up shoe laces and buttons, writing and threading beads.

7   Skills are developed which can then be transferred to everyday life, for example, getting in and out of a wheelchair, learning to count, sequencing. Some children may find it really hard to progress round the circuit, due perhaps to something as obvious as the inability to count. There may, however, be a concentration problem or a problem in the understanding of sequencing. This may be overcome in the classroom or by encouraging one of the more competent children to go round the circuit with the child who has the difficulty.

8   *Competition against Oneself is Encouraged*   The children are always trying to better their own scores and as they gradually improve, their confidence and determination increase, which in turn improves their performance.

Variations of the Circuit
1   The numbers of the exercises can be mixed up so that there is no logical sequence. This may help to improve sequencing skills, since the children must find the next number, wherever that may be.

2   The circuit can be graded into five colour grades, blue, red, black, silver and gold.

To determine your standards, when you begin the circuit, do a testing circuit to find out the highest and lowest scores of your particular group. The lowest score becomes the blue standard, the highest becomes the black; then calculate the red, silver and gold.

In one group, for example, the lowest score is two press-ups and five sit-ups (our blue standard). The highest score is eight press-ups and 20 sit-ups (our black standard). We calculate the other standards accordingly, as follows:

a	Blue	2 press-ups	5 sit-ups
b	Red	5 ,, ,,	10 ,, ,,
c	Black	8 ,, ,,	20 ,, ,,
d	Silver	10 ,, ,,	30 ,, ,,
e	Gold	15 ,, ,,	40 ,, ,,

Repeat the procedure for each of the exercises.

At each exercise place a card to show the required number of times the exercise must be done for a child to complete the given colour grade. Thus at 'Press-Ups' there will be a large, easily legible card which shows Blue as two, Red as five, Black as eight, etc.

You then place each child in a colour group, relevant to his ability. For example, Fred best fits into the Red group, so as he goes round the circuit he will always read what is required of him to achieve the Red standard. At 'Press-Ups' he must do five and at 'Sit-Ups' 10, and so on. When he has achieved the relevant score at each exercise, Fred has gained his Red Standard. He then starts to work for the Black.

The whole group is regularly re-assessed. On the colour circuit there is no time limit. However, on the testing circuit, when the children are being re-assessed, they are timed for about a minute in order to give a standard. The children will gradually progress up through the colour standards as they continue to improve their performance. Most children enjoy the challenge of aiming for a goal.

Additional Exercises

Exercises can be varied or added to your circuit according to the needs of the children in your particular group.

If the interdisciplinary team works well, it is possible for one member to suggest to the circuit organisers the inclusion of an exercise which might give added strength to a particular part of the body, which could in turn improve the child's performance in another discipline. For example, at the Cedar School, the swimming teacher asked if an exercise might be included in the circuit which would help to improve the swimming. We therefore added an exercise which involved sand bag lifting. This helped to strengthen the arm muscles and did a lot to improve the children's performance in the swimming pool.

Sandbag lift.

THE SKILLS CIRCUIT

The skills circuit was devised to improve the children's gross motor skills in preparation for playing team games. When we watched them we realised that they lacked most of the fundamental skills necessary for team games; indeed, their basic skills were very poor. They had:

No sense of direction
No awareness of space or team mates
No appreciation of score
No idea of the ball being in and out of play, of corners, goal kicks, offside
No ability to pick up the ball or to catch it
No ability to move with the ball
A basic fear of leaning from the wheelchair.

Some sort of training was obviously needed. With the circuit idea already off the ground, we then heard of the Football Association's Super Skills scheme. We wrote to the Association asking permission to adapt their scheme for our children. They agreed wholeheartedly and the Cedar Skills Circuit was devised.

The Football Association skills programme was a programme based on a badge system – Blue, Red, Black, Silver and Gold in increasing degrees of difficulty. There were seven basic skills and each was divided into the five categories. The Association agreed to allow us to award their badges on our adapted system. Like the FA scheme, ours includes seven exercises which can be modified to suit the particular needs of any group of children, the equipment needed being determined by the specific exercises chosen.

A large chart was made and displayed on the noticeboard so that every participating child could see which of the skills he had achieved and therefore which skills he needed to work on each week. In this way the children were encouraged to work out for themselves where they should be each session and were

NAME	blue	red	black	silver	gold
FRED					
ROSE					
BERT					

expected to move from skill to skill where vacancies occurred. There should be a maximum of two children to each skill if numbers and staff permit.

Obviously these decisions are not easy for the child with perceptual problems, but with encouragement and guidance and a clearly labelled system he will get the hang of the session fairly quickly.

Each skill is documented on individual charts as follows:

1

	Wheelchair	Walker	Electric Wheelchair
Blue	Pick up the ball round the wheel of your chair. Three times out of five.	Head a ball, thrown by a member of staff, three times in a row.	Memory Test. Copy five movements demonstrated by instructor while stationary, ie 'raise left arm'; 'turn head to left', etc., depending on ability of child.
Red	Pick up the ball five times out of five and score goal into space three metres by two metres at a distance of three metres.	Head ball thrown by member of staff into goal three metres by two metres at a distance of three metres. Staff stands three metres away. Three times out of five.	Ten movements copied as above.
Black	Hold a wheelie for ten seconds	As red award but five times out of five.	Copy seven movements, four stationary, three involving wheelchair manoeuvres.
Silver	Go over ramp five times.	Walk up onto platform and down other side (platform of kerb height).	Copy seven movements all wheelchair manoeuvres.
Gold	Wheelie over ramp with 360° turn at top three times.	Walk up onto platform, full turn and down, five times.	Copy fifteen manoeuvres – eight stationary, seven wheelchair.

2

	Wheelchair	Walker	Electric Wheelchair
Blue	Five throws and catches.	Five throws and catches.	Hanging target to be hit with any part of body or chair, three times consecutively.
Red	Ball thrown by staff member as diagram. Child catches three times out of five.	Ball thrown by staff member as diagram. Three catches out of five.	Hit target five times.
Black	As red but five times out of five.	As red but five times out of five.	Hit target seven times.
Silver	Wheelchair must turn and then child catch ball five times out of ten. Ball thrown by staff as in diagram.	Walker turns and then catches ball five times out of ten.	Hit target ten times.
Gold	As silver but ten times out of ten.	As silver but ten times out of ten.	Hit target fifteen times.

3

	Wheelchair	Walker	Electric Wheelchair
Blue	Bounce ball (basketball style), 20 times.	Bounce ball (basketball style), 20 times.	(Ball in net – suspended 30 cms away from wall) Punch ball to wall, 20 times. Height of ball is adjusted to suit each individual.
Red	Basketball bounce 30 times with left hand 30 times with right hand.	Basketball bounce 30 times with left hand 30 times with right hand.	Punch ball 30 times – if possible without stopping.
Black	Bounce ball round wheelchair. A double bounce at the back is acceptable.	Bounce ball round the body five times. Child stands still.	Punch ball 30 times with left hand 30 times with right hand.
Silver	Bounce ball in figure of eight with at least 20 bounces in each figure, five times.	Bounce ball in figure of eight, 20 bounces minimum, five times.	Punch ball 60 times with left hand 60 times with right hand.
Gold	Bounce ball round wheelchair 10 times. Double bounce at the back is acceptable.	Bounce ball in figure of eight as above, 15 times without stopping.	Punch ball 120 times with left hand 120 times with right hand.

4

	Wheelchair	Walker	Electric Wheelchair
Blue	←— 3m —→ Throw a ball five times out of 10 into bin.	←— 3m —→ Throw a ball five times out of 10 into bin 70 cms square.	Flik ball to box three metres distant four times out of 10. Box is 70 cms square.
Red	As blue but eight times out of 10.	As blue but eight times out of 10.	As blue but eight times out of 10.
Black	 Shooting three times out of five.	 Shooting three times out of five.	As red but decrease size of target to 30 cms square.
Silver	 Shooting seven times out of 10.	 Shooting seven times out of 10.	As black but five times out of five.
Gold	Basketball bounce across hall area, shoot into basket six times out of 10.	Basketball bounce across hall area, shoot into basket six times out of 10.	Using original target 10 times out of 10.

5

	Wheelchair	Walker	Electric Wheelchair
Blue	 To catch ball thrown by staff seven times out of 10.	 To catch ball thrown by staff seven times out of 10.	 5M (Equipment: Unihoc stick and puck plus goal). Dribble puck straight distance of five metres.
Red	 2m Either walker or wheelchair user can act as thrower in this skill. To catch seven times out of 10.	 2m Either walker or wheelchair user can act as thrower in this skill. To catch seven times out of 10.	 1m Shoot into Unihoc goal from distance of one metre three times out of five.
Black	As red but 10 times out of 10.	As red but 10 times out of 10.	 2m → shoot Dribble for two metres then shoot three times out of five.
Silver	 turn 3m Wheelchair must turn and catch from each end three times.	As silver for wheelchair, ie walker turns and catches from each end three times.	 Dribble puck between skittles three times.
Gold	As above 10 times without stopping.	As gold for wheelchair	 shoot Dribble and shoot five times out of five.
	(Electric wheelchair may use chair as 'stick' in all events if preferred).		

6

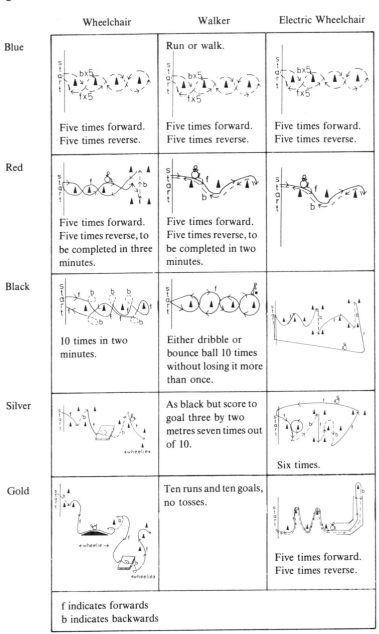

	Wheelchair	Walker	Electric Wheelchair
Blue	Five times forward. Five times reverse.	Run or walk. Five times forward. Five times reverse.	Five times forward. Five times reverse.
Red	Five times forward. Five times reverse, to be completed in three minutes.	Five times forward. Five times reverse, to be completed in two minutes.	
Black	10 times in two minutes.	Either dribble or bounce ball 10 times without losing it more than once.	
Silver		As black but score to goal three by two metres seven times out of 10.	Six times.
Gold		Ten runs and ten goals, no tosses.	Five times forward. Five times reverse.

f indicates forwards
b indicates backwards

7

	Wheelchair	Walker	Electric Wheelchair
Blue	wall ←1·25m→ 1m↕target ↑ 2m throwing line Throw a ball. Of 10 throws seven to hit target.	wall ←1·25m→ 1m↕target ↑ 2m throwing line Of 10 throws seven to hit target.	target Of five headers three to hit target on floor.
Red	Half size target 10 out of 10 to hit target.	Half size target 10 out of 10 to hit target.	As blue but five out of five to hit target.
Black	As blue but target on floor.	As blue but target on floor.	Half size target three out of five to hit target.
Silver	As red but target as black, ie on floor.	As red but target as black, ie on floor.	As black but five times out of five.
Gold	Quarter size target two metres distant on wall then on floor. 10 out of 10 hits on each target.	As gold for wheelchair.	Quarter size target seven times out of seven.

Conclusion

All the activities in the Circuit and the Skills Circuit are geared towards the improvement of gross motor skills. Proficiency in these skills will enable the child to develop his fine motor skills with a greater degree of competency – see page 62.

To many children most of the motor skills come naturally from everyday play – such as kicking, throwing, catching, playing in a team – but the handicapped child needs to be taught these skills in a systematic way.

The PE programme is only part of the child's whole curriculum and should not be viewed or performed in isolation. It is thus important to know with each child which skills he has and which he lacks. This can only be determined by discussion with all those involved with the child throughout the day. A checklist should be made for each child and regularly reviewed. For example, the taxi driver may point out that a certain child has difficulty in getting in and out of the taxi. This skill can then be looked at and analysed. The necessary skills (basically a sideways transfer, with its many variations) are then incorporated in the circuit.

If you are considering the education of the whole child, which must be the aim of every school, then PE is seen to be an essential part of the school curriculum.

5   Games for Handicapped Children

Physically handicapped children can get as much fun and enjoyment from games as any other children and, with a little thought and imagination, a wide range of games can be adapted to suit a given group. It is important to include all the children and to give them all something positive to do. A muscular dystrophy child confined to an electric wheelchair can manipulate his chair to guard a goal; he may not be able to hit the ball with his hands, but he can manoeuvre his chair so that a ball aimed at the goal bounces off it. He can also referee or time-keep (as in the circuit). In this chapter we are suggesting games that we have used successfully with our children. We have given rules and variations which suited our groups, but it may be necessary for you to adapt the rules slightly so as to suit your own particular group.

When playing games with physically handicapped children, one should bear in mind the following:

1   The children should be encouraged to take as active a part as is physically possible, but within the bounds of safety.
2   Rules can always be adapted to suit the children in any given group.
3   In any team game or relay, children of equal ability must, as far as possible, be put opposite one another.
4   When we have used the term to 'run' (as in non-stop cricket), we really mean to move as quickly as is possible for each individual.
5   Each member of the same team should be given a distinguishing coloured bib or band, since many children, especially at first, find it difficult to identify with the right team.
6   When we recommend that a large plastic ball should be used, we mean a light plastic ball of football size. If the children cannot manage with the suggested ball, it is always worth trying with a larger, lighter one, eg a beachball or a large foam ball.
7   When we suggest that 'goals' should be used, we mean the

ordinary five-a-side goals with nets when the game is played on a five-a-side pitch. In the hall, or for indoor games, we have found that a bench or form, turned on its side, makes a good goal.

8 In certain games or relays, it has been assumed that the children have a given skill – for example, in netball or handball it is assumed the children can throw a ball; in Relay B that they can get their arms above their heads. However if the children of your own group have not yet acquired the necessary skill, it is best to choose games for which they do have the skills (eg see the Numbers Game on page 83.

9 Distances can always be varied to suit the ability of your group of children.

10 There are a few basic safety rules which should always be taken into account.

a Children with lack of, or altered, sensation should either be on a friction-free floor or on mats to prevent pressure sores.

b In a game such as crab football, where the children move around a lot, all shoes, calipers, sticks and wheelchairs should be cleared from the playing area.

c If the children are playing with sticks, then certain safety rules must be observed, for example, the sticks must be kept below shoulder level and only used on the ball.

d In those games where the object is to touch another child with a ball it should be made clear that the balls used are lightweight foam, which cannot hurt.

11 When we use the word 'stands' (as in Non-Stop cricket, p 82) it is assumed that the children in wheelchairs will be sitting.

In order to try to help those with little experience of physically handicapped children, we have devised a grading system to suggest which games are suitable for particular children. We have divided the children into two groups:

a Wheelchair users =

b Walkers =

a   Wheelchair users

1   Is a paraplegic in a wheelchair or a very good wheelchair user who uses a wheelchair with a low back and no arms.

2   Is a good wheelchair user, ie uses a chair with no arms but with a back.

3   Fair wheelchair user, ie uses a wheelchair with arms and with a back.

4   A muscular dystrophy child in a wheelchair who uses padding and a belt.

5   Electric wheelchair user.

b   Walkers

1   Able-bodied child.

2   A child with minimal or no support.

3   A child with sticks and/or short calipers.

4   A child with sticks and above the knee calipers.

5   A child with sticks and pelvic band calipers.

6   A child with maximum support, ie rollator and/or high calipers.

INDOOR OR OUTDOOR GAMES

Against the Clock

Equipment
a   Cut-down netball or basketball posts.
b   Plastic ball for each of the players in one team.
c   Skittles to make a slalom course.

Aim
For Team A to score as many baskets as possible in the time it takes for Team B to complete the slalom course.

Organisation
a   Have two teams of four to ten players of similar ability – who must be able to throw.
b   Team A stand in a semi-circle around the goal post.
c   Team B stand in a line two metres away from the slalom course.

Rules
a   Team A take it in turns to try to score baskets.
b   A teacher or a player returns the balls to the players.
c   In the meantime team B has to complete the slalom course, each player in turn.
d   When all of team B have completed the slalom course, team A count up the baskets scored.
e   The teams change over. The winning team is the team which scores most baskets.

Variations

Vary the targets used by team 'A'.
   (i)   Throw bean bags into a bin.

(ii)   Throw bean bags at a target.

(iii)   Knock over skittles with a ball.

(iv)   Throw bean bags against a board with holes in it. Each hole carries a different score.

(v)   Instead of scoring baskets team A can score a point by moving from one line across ten metres and back.

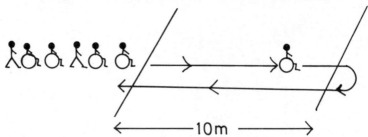

The distance can be varied according to the ability of the children taking part.

(vi)   Team A can score by individually bringing bean bags from a pile, several metres from the base.

(vii) Team A can build towers with a given number of blocks, all working to complete a tower at the same time.

Balloon Ball

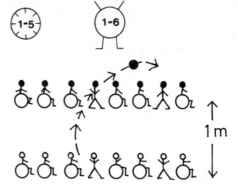

Equipment

One balloon.

Aim

To score a point by hitting the balloon on to the floor behind the line of players' chairs.

Organisation

a   Have two teams of an equal number of players.

b   Team A sit in a line facing team B about one metre apart.

Rules
a   The referee throws the balloon into the air.
b   The players try to hit the balloon over the opponents' heads so that it hits the floor behind their chairs. A point is then scored.
c   The winning team scores most points!

Variations
a   A goal can be put at either end of the teams. To score, the balloon must be batted with the hand into the goal.
b   Using the same formation but no balloon, make a pile of objects at one end of the line. Pass them one at a time to the other end. The game then can become a relay between the two teams and the first team to pass all the objects wins.
c   The relay becomes more difficult if the objects are passed up to the opposite end in front, and then at the same time passed back to the original end, behind the players' backs. The first team to get all the objects to one end and back wins.

Circle Tag

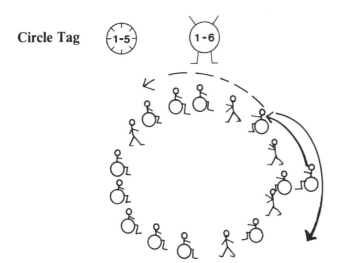

Equipment
None!

Aim
To reach the empty space before the opponent.

Organisation
All the children form a circle and are paired off according to ability.

Rules
a   Each child of a pair is given the same number.
b   When a number is called, the two children with that number go round the outside of the circle.
c   The first child back wins.
d   The game begins again, with another number.

Crab Football

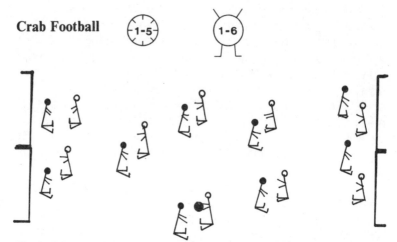

Equipment
a   Two very wide goals, eg two benches across the room.
b   Ball.
Aim
To score a goal by hitting the ball against the face of the bench.
Organisation
a   Have two teams of four to ten players each, placed strategically across the court in pairs (one from each team) on the floor.
b   Throw the ball into the middle.
Rules
a   The players move across the floor, however they can, and hit the ball however they can – with the hand, head, feet or elbows – towards the bench of the opposing team.
b   No player must get up.
Variations
a   Mark the court into areas. Pair off the children with similar disability (one from each team) and confine them to one area of the room.

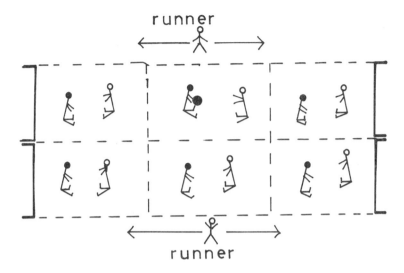

b   Put runners up the side of the court to feed the ball back in.
c   Restrict players to mats (particularly if the children with altered sensation are playing).
d   Electric wheelchair users can be goalies or runners.

Dodge Ball

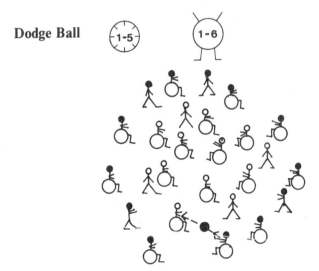

Equipment
One large foam ball.

Aim

For the players in team A to hit the players of team B below the waist or, in the case of wheelchair users, on the front small wheels, so causing them to be out.

Organisation

a   Have two teams of an equal number of players.

b   The players in team A form a circle. Team B stand or sit inside the circle formed by team A.

Rules

a   Team A has the ball which they then aim, to hit the players of team B below the waist, or wheelchair users on the small front wheels. Any player from team B who is hit is then out. Play continues until all of team B are out. The teams then change over.

Variations

a   The teams can be timed. The winning team gets the opponents out in the fastest time (an electric wheelchair user can be timer).

b   A time limit can be given. The winning team gets the most opponents out.

Non-Stop Cricket

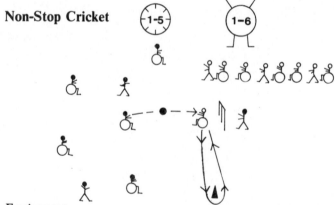

Equipment

a   Cricket stump, ideally with springs (or a chair or box to use as a stump).

b   Skittle/box/chair.

Aim

For the batsman to make runs for his team by running around the skittle without being out. The team with the most runs wins.

Organisation
a   Have two teams of four to ten players of similar ability.
b   One team bats, the other fields.
c   The batting team stands clear of the pitch behind the stumps, except the first batsman who stands in front of the stumps.
d   The fielders are strategically placed around the pitch. One fielder is the bowler and stands three to four metres opposite the first batsman in line with the stumps. One fielder acts as backstop behind the stumps.

Rules
a   The bowler bowls the ball to the first batsman.
b   The batsman tries to hit the ball. Whether he hits or misses, he must run round the skittle and back to the stumps.
c   Meanwhile the fielders must get the ball back to the bowler who must *immediately* bowl again (no matter where the batsman is).
d   If the bowler hits the stumps or the batsman is caught, he is out. The second batsman takes his place *as quickly as possible* because *as soon as* the bowler gets the ball, he will bowl *immediately*. If the bowler hits the stumps before the second batsman gets into place, in front of the stumps, he is out and the third batsman goes in.
e   If the batsman hits the ball so well that he can run round the skittle several times, eg five, before the bowler retrieves the ball and is able to bowl again, the batsman gets that many runs (five).

Numbers Game

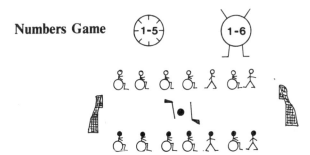

Equipment
a   One large plastic ball.
b   Two Unihoc sticks (one for each team).
c   Two goals – one at each end.

Aim

To score a goal by knocking the ball with the stick into the goal of the opposing team.

Organisation

a   Have two teams with an equal number of players (any number within reason!) The teams must pair reasonably well, eg a child with dystrophy in one team must be opposite a dystrophy in the other.

b   The teams line up on either side of the court.

c   Give a number to each player. Each number must have a counterpart in the opposing team.

d   Place the ball in the middle with a Unihoc stick on either side.

e   There is no goalkeeper.

Rules

a   The referee calls out a number.

b   The two players from each team, who have that number, pick up a stick and try to hit the ball into the goal with it.

c   It is a good idea to make clear before the start of the game which stick belongs to which team.

d   The sticks must only be used to hit the ball. A free hit is awarded to the opposing player for dangerous play.

Variations

a   The ball may be kicked, instead of using sticks.

b   The players may pick up the ball and throw it.

c   A bean bag may be used instead of the ball.

d   Very handicapped children can go in goal or act as barriers on the way down. An electric wheelchair user can defend the goal.

Rounders

Equipment

a   Medium light ball, such as a 30 cm diameter plastic ball.

b   Longer, lighter bat than normally used.

c   Four bases and base for bowler and one for the batsman.

Aim

To score a rounder by running round four bases as in rounders.

Organisation

a   Two teams of seven players.

b   The batting team stands in a line behind the pitch.
c   The fielders are placed as in rounders. With severely handicapped children, they would be placed as in diagram.

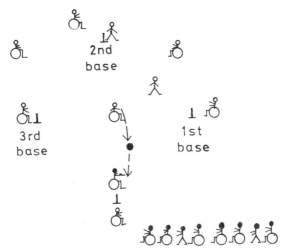

Rules
As for rounders.

Variations

a   Use larger ball and longer lighter bat.
b   For those who cannot hold a bat, the ball can bounce off the wheelchair. Those wheelchair users who cannot propel themselves can be pushed.

Scooter Boards

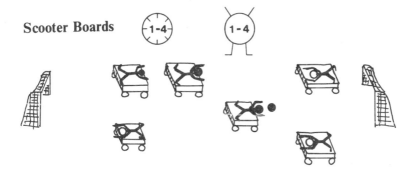

Equipment
a   Scooter board per player.
b   Large plastic ball.
c   Goals, or benches on their sides to be used as goals.
Aim
To score a goal by hitting the ball into the goal or against the face of the bench.
Organisation
a   Two teams of three to six players, each of whom lies on his tummy on a scooter board.

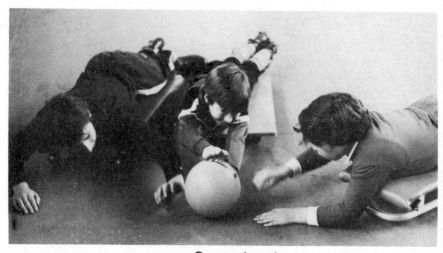

Scooter boards.

b   The ball is put in the middle of the pitch.
Rules
a   On the referee's whistle the players move on the scooter boards towards the ball.
b   The players hit the ball with their hands towards the opposing goal.
c   No player is allowed to grab at another. A free pass is given against any offender.

Human Cricket

Equipment
One plastic ball.

Aim
To score a run by running from one line across to the other.
Organisation
a Two teams of five or more players.
b One team lines up behind, but along, one line.
c One player comes forward as the batsman.
d The fielding team spread out between the first line and the second.
e One player is the bowler, who stands in the middle.

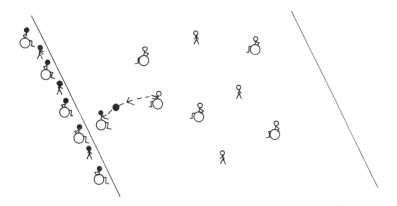

Rules
a The bowler bowls the ball to the batsman.
b He hits it or kicks it in any way he can.
c Then all his team try to move from the first line across to the second. As they try to cross, the fielding team try to touch them with the ball.
d All players who are touched by the ball are out.
e Each one who crosses the second line without being touched scores a run.
f The bowler then turns and bowls to a second batsman who will hit the ball for all the team now standing behind the second line. He continues until all the batsmen are out.
g Children in wheelchairs are out if a specified part of the wheelchair is hit by the ball.
h The teams change over and the team with the highest number of runs wins the game.

Stoolball

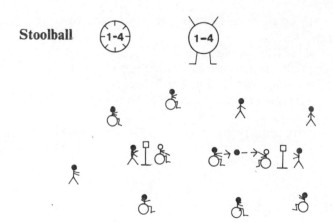

Equipment
a Two boards, each one foot square, mounted on poles approximately four feet from the ground (needs to be shorter for wheelchair users) and 16 yards apart.
b Ball.
c At least two bats.

Aim
a For the batsman to score runs by running between the boards (as cricket).
b For the bowler to hit the board causing the batsman to be out.

Organisation
a Two teams of at least eleven players of similar ability.
b The batting team waits off the pitch except for two batsmen who stand, one in front of each board.
c The fielders are placed around the pitch. One fielder bowls from the middle of the pitch. A backstop stands behind the boards.

Rules
a From the middle, the bowler bowls two balls to a batsman at one end, trying to hit the target.
b He then bowls two balls to the batsman at the other end.
c In the meantime the batsman tries to hit the ball and both batsmen then run between the targets (as in cricket).

d   The batsman is out if:
   (i)   The bowled ball hits the target.
   (ii)   The ball is caught off his bat, hand or wrist.
   (iii)   If he is run out.
e   The batsman scores a run each time he runs between the targets. A ball which reaches the boundary gives him four runs. If he hits the ball straight over the boundary, he gets six runs.
f   The team with the most runs wins (as in cricket).

Volleyball

Equipment
a   Small volleyball court.
b   Lower net than normal.
c   Volleyball.
Aim
To score a goal by causing the ball to touch the floor of the opposing court.
Organisation
Two teams of six players sit on opposing sides of the net, as in volleyball.
Rules
Played according to the normal rules of volleyball.

Variations

a   Use a bench across the middle instead of a net. Increase the number of players. Use a beach ball. Allow one bounce either side of the net.

b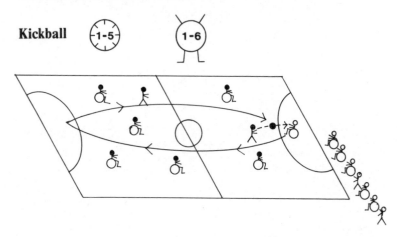

Put staff and electric wheelchair users at the back of the court to feed the ball back into play.

c Put electric wheelchair users at the front of the court to head the ball, or to deflect it by allowing it to rebound from the chair.

d Vary the size of the pitch according to the severity of handicap.

GAMES PLAYED WITHIN A FIVE-A-SIDE FOOTBALL PITCH AREA

Kickball

Equipment
One large soft ball.
Aim
To make runs by moving from one base to the other and back again.
Organisation
a Have two teams of four to ten players each, with roughly the same ability.
b One team bats, while the other fields.
c The batting team stand in a line behind the base on the right.
d The fielders are placed strategically over the court.

Rules
a   The batting side come forward one at a time.
b   The bowler from the fielding team bowls or rolls the ball to the first batsman who kicks, punches, or heads it into the playing area.
c   If the ball is caught by a fielder before it touches the ground, the whole batting team is out.
d   If the ball lands outside the playing area, the first batsman is out and batsman two goes in to bat.
e   If the ball lands inside the playing area, the batsman must get to the base at the other end of the pitch, where he can stay, or he can try to return to the first base.
f   As the batsman crosses the court, the fielding side try to touch him with the ball below the knee (or the waist if preferred), or to hit the front of the wheelchair.
g   Fielders are not allowed to run with the ball, but when they are in possession of it they can either aim it at the batsman or pass it to someone else who can then aim it.
h   The teams change over when all the batsmen are out.

Football

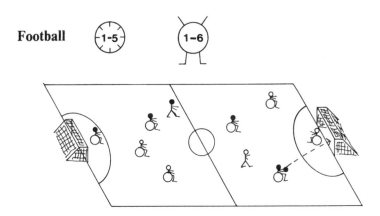

Equipment
a   Five-a-side pitch.
b   Goals and nets (if possible).
c   Light plastic ball.
Aim
To score goals for your team by getting the ball into the net.

Football.

Organisation
Two teams of five to ten strategically placed on the pitch.
Rules
a Normal football rules, except that . . .
b . . . players in wheelchairs are allowed to handle the ball.
Once a wheelchair player has the ball in his lap, he is allowed
only two pushes and must then pass the ball.
Variations
a If a wheelchair user touches the ball with his hand, nobody
else is allowed to stop him from picking it up.
b Only the goalkeeper is allowed in the goal areas.
c Very heavily handicapped children can be included by
using them as goalkeepers.

Netball

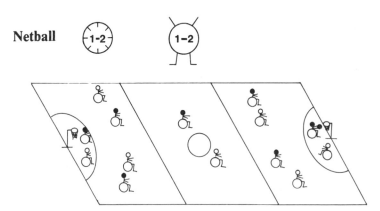

Equipment
a Five-a-side pitch.
b Netball posts cut down.
c Plastic ball.
Aim
To score a goal by shooting the ball through the net on the
posts.
Organisation
a Two teams of five to ten players strategically placed on the
court.
Rules
As for netball.

Rugby Pass

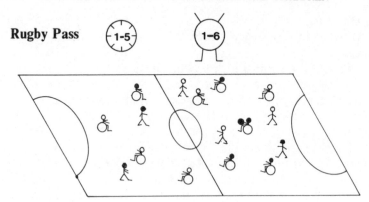

Equipment
a   Plastic ball.
b   Five-a-side football pitch.
Aim
To touch a player of the opposing team with the ball.
Organisation
a   Have two teams of four to ten players. If there are five in a team use half of a five-a-side pitch. With ten in a team, the whole pitch would be used.
b   Team A is in possession of the ball.
c   Team B is trying to escape.
Rules
a   Team A pass the ball.
b   The player with the ball is not allowed to move with it, but must try to get the ball near enough to a player in team B to touch him with it.
c   As soon as a player is touched, the teams change over and team A now try to escape.

Touch Ball

Equipment
a   Five-a-side pitch.
b   Large plastic ball.
Aim
To put the ball down in the touch-down area behind the opponents' goal line (as in rugby).

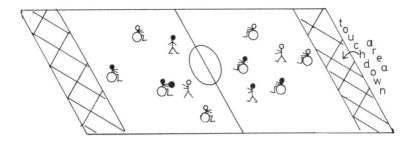

Organisation
a   Have two teams of four to ten players placed on the pitch in pairs.
Rules
a   The referee puts the ball in the centre.
b   Team A begin by passing the ball in any direction to get it near the opponents' touch line.
c   There is *no* tackling. To win the ball a player must touch an opponent who is in possession of it. If A touches B, B must give the ball to A and move three feet away.
Variations
a   With an academically good group the ball must be passed backwards as in rugby.

Mat Ball

Equipment
a   Five-a-side pitch.
b   Two mats or two bins.
c   One large plastic ball.
Aim
To score a goal by getting the ball either into the opponents' bin, or onto their mat.
Organisation
Two teams of four to ten players each, placed across the pitch.
Rules
a   The referee throws the ball into the middle of the pitch.
b   The players must then try to get the ball and put it
    (i)   into the opponents' bin, or

(ii)   onto the opponents' mat by passing the ball in any way possible. The player must not move when in possession of the ball.

c   Electric wheelchair users can guard the bin or mat.

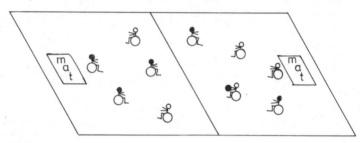

Variations

Players can move with the ball.

Handball

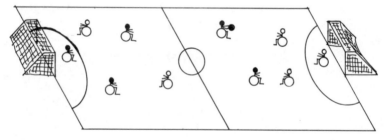

Equipment

a   Five-a-side pitch.

b   Goals and nets (if possible).

c   Light plastic ball.

Aim

To score a goal by getting the ball into the net.

Organisation

Two teams of five to ten strategically placed on the pitch.

Rules

a   The same as for football except that the ball is thrown, not kicked.

b   The wheelchair user can carry the ball in his lap for three consecutive pushes. Then he must pass the ball or shoot for goal.

c   It is a foul if a player knocks the ball from another's lap. A free throw is awarded against the offender.

Variations

a

There is a mixed team of wheelchair users and able-bodied children. The able-bodied must pass at least once to a wheelchair user before a goal can be scored.

b   *Indoor handball*   Similar to handball except that instead of nets at either end of the court there is, *either*
   (i)   a member of staff standing on a bench, *or*
   (ii)   a heavily handicapped child in a wheelchair going backwards and forwards in front of the bench, *or*
   (iii)   the goalkeeper is on the same side and his team play *towards* him.

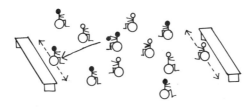

To score a goal, *either*
   (i)   the goalkeeper standing on the bench must catch the ball thrown to him by his team mates, *or*
   (ii)   the team must touch any part of the wheelchair or person in it. In this case use a soft foam ball.

Hockey

Equipment
a   Five-a-side pitch.
b   Hockey stick per player (children with sticks can use own stick). Wheelchair users have shorter sticks.
c   Large plastic ball.
d   Goals and nets (if possible).

Aim
To score a goal by hitting the ball into the net.

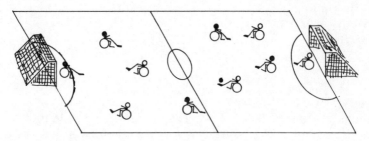

Organisation
a   Two teams of five to ten players of similar ability, strategically placed round the pitch.
Rules
a   The same as for hockey.
b   It is most important to keep the sticks below shoulder height otherwise it is dangerous.
Variations

a   *Unihoc*

Played with plastic sticks which are lighter, and with a plastic puck or Unihoc ball. This enables more heavily handicapped children to play. The rules are as for hockey.
b   *Shinty*   Use walking sticks upside down.

Basketball

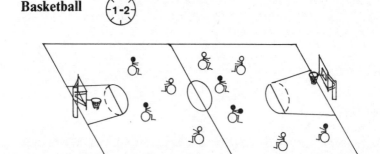

Equipment
a   Basketball court (ideally 26 metres × 14 metres).
b   Ring (45 cms in diameter) fixed to a backboard 1·20 m ×

Basketball.

1·80 m which is 3·05 m above the ground. The backboard should be of solid material.

c   Basketball ball.

d   Stop watch.

Aim

To throw the ball into the opponents' basket.

Organisation

Two teams of up to ten players of whom five from each team are on the court at one time.

Rules

The rules are as set out by the International Stoke Mandeville Games Federation.

Variations

a   The ring can be adjustable, allowing children to play who are less able to throw (see diagrams overleaf).

b   A lighter ball which has a similar bounce can be used.

c   More players can be put in each team.

d   Use two or three balls at one time.

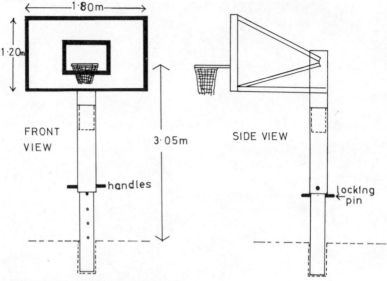

ADJUSTABLE BASKETBALL NET

In games such as basketball, handball, football, etc., as well as using skills learnt in the skills circuit (see page 64), the children must learn certain skills which are ideally learnt in the game situation, such as:

(i)   Playing in a team.
(ii)   Direction of play.
(iii)   Being able to identify your own team members.
(iv)   Moving into a space to receive a ball.

However, as you play the game, you will realise that certain moving skills need working on. It is possible to isolate these skills and to teach them in small groups, eg:

1   To get the ball.
2   To keep the ball.
3   If you lose the ball, how to get it back.

To achieve 1, the children are put into groups of four and given a ball, and play two against two. The two with the ball have to see how many times they can pass it before they lose it to the other two. To achieve skill 2, put the children into groups of five, three against two. The group of three should always be able to keep the ball by passing from one to the other. To achieve 3, put the children into groups of four, two against two. Each attacking player closely marks his opposite number in an attempt to intercept the ball when it is passed. To improve the marking skill, you can also put the children into pairs. One tries to escape from the other one at a given signal. When the whistle is blown a short while later, the children stop dead and the marker sees if he can touch his opponent.

As you play the games it will become apparent that other skills will need to be isolated and broken down in a similar way:

(i)   In basketball it is often necessary to change direction quickly at any given moment. This can be practised.

(ii)   The individual can practise throwing the ball straight in front of him with a backward spin. This enables him to do two pushes, throw the ball, do two more pushes and then retrieve the ball he has thrown.

In Any Game played on a Five-a-side Pitch

The pitch can be divided into areas. In each area put two children of a similar handicap, one from each team, and confine them to it. In this way, the game is not dominated by the most able children.

RELAYS

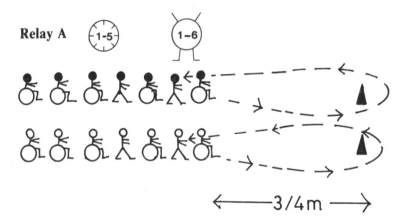

Relay A

a   Two teams line up.

b   A skittle is placed three to four metres (can be varied depending on the ability of the group) in front of the line.

c The first in the team goes round the skittle and back to his place.

d He touches the second in the team who goes round the skittle, and so on until all have had a turn.

e The first team to complete the exercise wins.

Relay B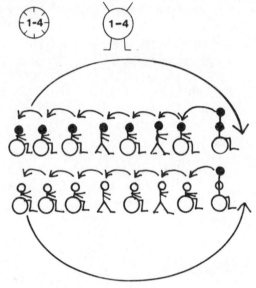

a Two teams line up, one behind the other.

b The first child passes a ball overhead to the second one, and so on to the back one who comes to the front and repeats the process.

c The first team to finish wins.

Variations

a Use a progressively smaller ball until a bead can be used.

b Sit the children side by side and pass the ball from lap to lap. In this variation a dystrophy child can be included. The last child gets up and goes to the other end of the line and the process is repeated.

Relay C   In and Out Relays

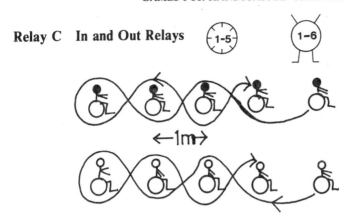

a   Two teams line up, each child standing one metre from the next.
b   The first child weaves in and out of the team and comes back to his place.
c   He touches the second child who then weaves in and out of *all* the team and back to his place, and so on.

Relay D   Potato Races

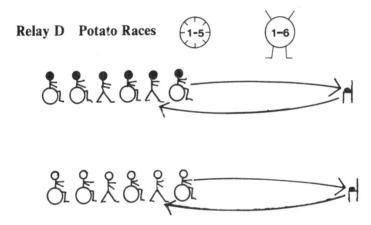

a   Two teams line up one behind the other.
b   A bean bag is put on a chair three to four metres away.
c   A runs to the chair, picks up the bean bag and brings it back to B who puts it back on the chair.
d   C brings it back to D who replaces it on the chair, and so on.

e   Someone can place the bean bag on an electric wheelchair user's lap.

f   Children who use two sticks can wear a bag round their necks to carry the bean bag in.

Relay E   Ball round the Team

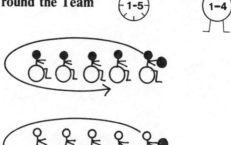

a   Two teams line up, one behind the other.

b   A at the front takes a ball all the way round the team and gives it to B who does the same, and so on.

c   Wheelchair users can take the ball on their lap.

d   Children with sticks can either hit it with their stick or carry it in a bag round their neck.

e   Walkers can kick it or carry it.

Relay F   Dressing Relay

To encourage those with dressing problems.

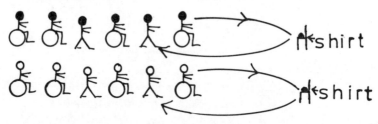

a   Two teams line up, one behind the other.

b   A shirt is placed on a chair three metres in front of the team.

c   A must go to the chair, put on the shirt, do up one button, come back to his place, take the shirt off, give it to B who puts it on, does up one button, goes to the chair where he places the shirt, and so on.

Variations
a   Use a hat, gloves, jumper or all four!
b   Each player in the team can be given a shirt (or jumper, hat, etc.). The winning team is the team which gets dressed first.

Relay G   Tunnel Ball

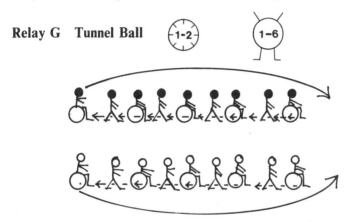

a   Two teams line up, one behind the other, a wheelchair user and a walker alternating.
b   A small ball is then passed under the wheelchairs and through the legs of the walkers, from the front to the back.
c   The last child in the team picks up the ball and takes it to the front of the line, where the process is repeated until each child has had a turn.

Relay H   Objects Relay

Have two teams of equal numbers. At one end of each team place a pile of ten objects, eg bean bags. At a given signal, A begins to pass the objects along the line, one after another, as quickly as possible. As soon as one object reaches the other end of the line, it has to be passed back. The first team to pass all the objects down one way and back to the beginning to form a pile again wins.

Relay I

Have two teams of equal numbers, sitting on the floor, well spread out. The leader has a hoop which he must get through and then pass on to the second player, and so on until all in the team have passed through the hoop.

Relay J

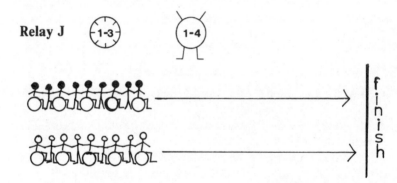

Have two teams of equal numbers in a line, each child holding on to the one in front. The team moves along towards a given goal. If anyone lets go, the whole team has to stop. The child at the back stays still and the team reassembles until everyone is once again holding on, when they again begin to move forwards. The team to reach the goal first, wins.

GAMES FOR YOUNGER CHILDREN
(enjoyed even by Seniors!)

Musical Games
A variety of musical games can be enjoyed by physically handicapped children.

1 *Musical Bumps*
While the music plays, the children move around the room. As soon as it stops, the children sit down on the floor. The last to sit down is out. The game continues until only one child is left in – the winner.

2 *Musical Mats*
Several small mats or sheets of newspaper are put down on the floor at intervals around the centre of the room. While the music plays the children move around the outside of the room. As soon as the music stops the children go and stand on a mat as quickly as possible. The last one to step on a mat is out. A wheelchair user has only to get part of a wheel on the mat.

3 *Musical 'Freeze'*
While the music plays, the children move around the room. As soon as the music stops they 'freeze'. The last to 'freeze' is out. Also, anyone who moves before the music begins again is out. Children in wheelchairs can play equally well.

4 *Musical Pile*
Place a pile of objects, eg bean bags, in the centre of the room. There must be one less than the number of players. Mark out a route round the outside of the room with skittles. The players move around this route while the music plays. When it stops, the players move to grab an object from the pile. The player who fails to get one is out. Next time round have one less object and so on until there are two players left and one object. The player who finally grabs the object is the winner. If children in wheelchairs are playing, place the objects on a table.

5 *Musical Grab*
Place a pile of different coloured objects, eg eight red ones, six blue ones, ten yellow, eight green, etc., in the centre of the room. While the music plays the children move around the outside of the room. As soon as the music stops a colour, eg red, is called out. The children move to the pile and pick up something red. Anyone who fails to pick up a red object is out. next time round a different colour is called out. As fewer children are left in the requirements are defined in greater detail, eg a large soft yellow object, until only one child remains.

Variations
Use different coloured shapes and call out a shape. When only

a few children are left, make it more difficult by defining the shape in greater detail, eg a small yellow square.

6 *Musical Numbers*

While the music plays the children move around. As soon as the music stops a number is called out, eg three. The children then put themselves into groups of three. Any children who are not in a group of three are out. Each time the music stops a different number is called out, until two children are left – the joint winners.

7 *Lucky Musical Numbers*

Place around the room large pieces of card with numbers (from one to six) written on them. While the music plays the children move around. When the music stops the children choose a number and stand by it. A large dice is rolled. The number which comes out, for example, six, determines who is out. In this case all those who went to the number six are out. As fewer children remain in the game the number cards should be removed. When there are only three left, the children are told that they must all go to different numbers until one child is left.

Variations

Use names of cities or colours, shapes, card suits, etc., on the cards. The referee holds copies of the cards chosen, shuffles them and chooses a different one each time.

Games of All Kinds

1 *Blindfold Listen and Guess*

Divide the children into four teams: red, yellow, blue and green, and put each team into a corner of the room. One member from each team goes into the middle of the room and is blindfolded, and turned around three times. At a given signal the teams all call out their own colour (and nothing else) to guide their team member back to the team. The first one back wins.

2 *Simon Says*

One child goes to the front of the room and faces the rest of the children. He gives them a series of orders: 'Simon says, "open your mouth",' 'Simon says, "touch your ear".' The children do as he says. Should he omit 'Simon says' and merely say 'Open your mouth', the children must not do as the leader says. Anyone who does is out. The game should obviously be adjusted to the group playing. As the children become more competent, so the leader can speed up his orders or mislead the group by performing actions which should not be imitated, and so on.

3   *Corner Swop*

The four teams are each in a corner of the room. At a given signal they have to swop corners diagonally so team A changes with D and B changes with C.

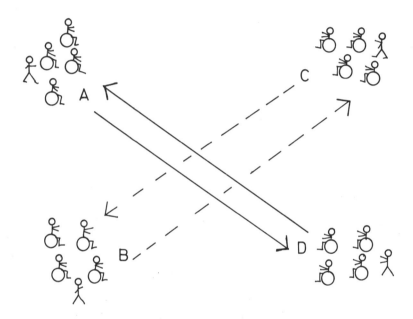

4   *Hands Down*

The children sit in a circle on the floor. One child sits in the middle. Four pieces of chalk are given separately to four different children in the circle. The children then pass the pieces of chalk, or pretend to pass them. When the child in the centre says, 'Hands down', all those in the circle put their hands on the floor, attempting to hide the chalk while the child in the centre tries to guess who has a piece of chalk. If the guess is correct the child in the centre changes places with the child who has the chalk. If after three guesses the child in the centre still has not picked a winner, the chalk is passed round again before he tries again.

Variations

It is not necessary to put the hands down on the floor. The children can hold clenched fists out in front of them.

5 *Throwing for Distance*

Each child in a group throws a balloon as far as he can. The one who throws farthest is the winner. Instead of a balloon the children could use a medicine ball, plastic ball, or a beach ball, depending on ability.

6 *What's the time, Mr Wolf?*

One child stands out in front of the rest of the group who stand against the opposite wall of the room. The group call out 'What's the time, Mr Wolf?' If he says '3 o'clock', everyone takes three steps towards 'Mr Wolf'. If he says '8 o'clock' they all take eight steps. If a child can reach Mr Wolf they change places and the game begins again. If Mr Wolf answers 'dinner time' he then chases after those in the group and tries to catch one of them before they get back to the wall. The child who is caught takes Mr Wolf's place.

Variations

The children creep up on Mr Wolf without talking. Every so often Mr Wolf turns round; if he sees anyone moving that child must return to the wall and begin again. When a child reaches Mr Wolf they change places and the game begins again.

7 *Tunnel Target*

The children form a circle with their legs apart. One child stands in the middle with a ball. He has three minutes during which time he must score as many goals as possible. A goal is scored if he succeeds in getting the ball through someone's legs or by touching the footplates of a wheelchair. Staff would have to pass the ball back to the child in the centre following each attempt. After three minutes a different child goes into the middle and tries his luck.

8 *Holey Board*

Have a large board with holes in it. Each hole represents a given score written on the board by the hole. Each child aims a given number of bean bags or balls, eg six, through the holes. For each ball which goes through a hole, the child receives that score, which is totalled.

9 *Shuttle Board*

Have a board 2 m × 0·5 m. At one end the board is divided into compartments by wooden strips. Each compartment has a given score. Each child aims a given number of wooden discs, eg ten, into the compartments and totals his score.

10 *Shove Halfpenny*

A board 61 cm × 37 cm is divided off into ten sections by lines running across the board. One line 32 mm from and parallel to each edge runs at right angles to them and marks the edges of the scoring area. Each player has five circular discs. He aims his halfpenny between the lines and when he gets one completely between two lines he marks off a score at the side. The first player to shove three 'halfpennies' between each of the nine parallel lines wins.

11 *British Bulldog*

Children line up along line A except one child who is the 'British Bulldog'. He stands in the centre of the playing area. At a given signal the children rush from line A towards line B. The 'British Bulldog' attempts to catch them. When he touches someone,

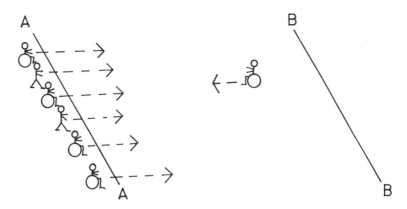

he remains still and the 'British Bulldog' must say, 'One, two, three, British Bulldog'. If the 'British Bulldog' forgets the words the child who was caught is free to go. If he does remember the words, the tagged child becomes another 'British Bulldog'. The winner is the last child to be tagged.

6 Sports in which Handicapped Children Can Take Part

Handicapped children can take part in the sports listed on the following pages. Any modifications we have found necessary are mentioned, but each teacher may find it necessary slightly to adapt a sport to suit the children in his group. Unless a sport is obviously impossible for a child (eg a child with advanced dystrophy could not do archery) then it is worth a try, even if it has to be modified. For instance, volleyball on a full-size court may be impossible for your group, but on a smaller court, with a lower net and a lighter ball, 'volleyball' can provide a great deal of enjoyment for handicapped children. It is essential that a well qualified instructor is in control, particularly in the potentially more dangerous sports, such as canoeing, rowing and yachting. For although the children need a challenge which means they must be stretched to their limits, the challenge must be controlled by someone who not only completely understands the demands of the sport but also the limitations of the individual children.

INDOOR AND OUTDOOR SPORTS
1 Archery
Some thirty per cent of all right-handed people have a dominant left eye and fifty per cent of all left-handed people are right eye dominant. This creates only a small mental problem to the able-bodied child who merely has to overcome the initial thought of doing it the 'wrong way round'. However, the problem may be much more difficult to overcome for a handicapped child whose disability may prevent him from shooting according to his dominant eye.

This is due to the effects of tension and compression to which the body is subjected when shooting. Half of the upper body (ie hand, wrist, arm, shoulders and chest) is under compression when using the bow, and the other half (including the fingers of the hand that is pulling on the bowstring) is under tension. A physically handicapped child may suffer pain if he shoots from one particular side but not from the other. For example, the disability of a physically handicapped child may make it necessary for him to shoot left-handedly when his dominant eye would suggest that he should shoot in a right-handed manner. Hence basic archery rules may have to be adapted to take account of a given disability. The teacher will have to decide whether the child's disability should override the 'dominant eye' rule. He may also have to adapt the child's position when shooting, to accommodate some inherent weakness.

In the photograph on p 114 of the boys at 'full draw' (ie at the point when they have to shoot) various points are clearly illustrated.

The boy in the foreground, Russell, has adopted the classic position. That is, the elbow of the drawing hand is at the same height as the shoulder on the right hand side and the top finger of the bow hand is at the same height as the shoulder on the left side.

The second boy, Mark, has to raise his right elbow higher; this is because of restricted movement in his right wrist which prevents him from holding his bow at the generally accepted level.

The third boy, Robin, also holds his elbow too high. In his case this is due to perceptual problems.

These three boys are all right-handed with dominant right eyes. They are therefore all right-handed archers.

The fourth boy, Paul, however, is left-eye dominant, but because compression causes him pain in his left wrist, he had to be taught to shoot right-handed, but with his left eye closed. Archers are normally taught to shoot with both eyes open.

Because many children with spina bifida have a reduced straight length of spine, they have to shoot without the side arm rest on their wheelchairs, so that there is string clearance. This is illustrated by Sara.

Variations
a   Cross-bow archery.
b   Darchery. The target is a dart board, rather than the usual target.
c   Field Archery. The archer shoots into the distance, onto a target sited on the ground.

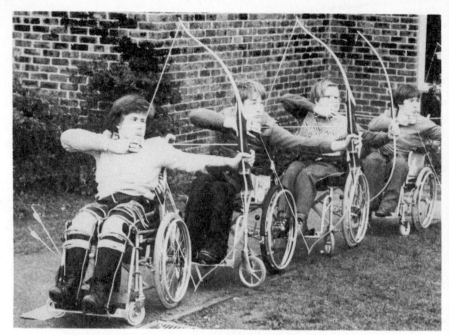

Archery. A team of boys at 'full draw'.

Archery. Sara, a spina bifida pupil, shoots without her arm rest, to accommodate her reduced spine length.

2 Badminton

The size of the court can be reduced and the net lowered, or wheelchair users can play near the net with able-bodied players covering the back of the court. More able players can play on a full size court on one side of the net, while less able players play on a smaller court on the other.

3 Bar Billiards

4 Billiards and Snooker

5 Bowls

6 Croquet

7 Curling

An indoor set can now be bought suitable for people in wheelchairs. A special mat is unrolled to cover the floor.

8 Darts

The height of the board may need to be reduced.

9 Electronic Games

These may be very beneficial to the heavily handicapped who can here compete on equal terms with other children.

10 Fencing

The wheelchairs have to be locked to the floor in a special frame (see the International Stoke Mandeville Games Federation Rules).

11 Golf

12 Horseshoe Pitching

13 Lawn Darts

14 Pétanque

15 Pistol Shooting

16 Rifle Shooting

17 Shove Halfpenny – See page 111.

18   Shuffle Board

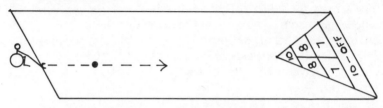

The child stays behind a line and pushes a puck with a shuffle stick into the triangle to score.

19   Shuttle Board – See page 110.

20   Skittles

21   Table Tennis
Children must be equally matched, ie wheelchair users play others in wheelchairs. If a child is in a wheelchair he should not be allowed to put his feet on the ground, for this gives him an unfair advantage – see the International Stoke Mandeville Games Federation Rules.

22   Ten Pin Bowling

23   Weight Lifting
This pursuit is for older children. For competition weight lifting see the International Stoke Mandeville Games Federation Rules.

24   Weight Training

OUTDOOR PURSUITS
See the 'Human Horizon' books *Out of Doors with Handicapped People* and *Outdoor Adventure for Handicapped People* by Mike Cotton.

1   Camping
'A' pole tents or tents with no inside poles are more suitable for wheelchair users. Toilet facilities should be checked before choosing a site. Plenty of helpers, usually including a nurse, are necessary. The children should be involved as much as

Camping – using
an 'A' pole tent.

The joys of camping!

possible. To organise the camp along scouting lines (ie with small groups of children allocated to various duties on a rota basis) is a well tested method. It is important to put the children into well balanced groups so that all the severely handicapped children are not put together. Also make sure that the more able do not monopolise but give the less able a chance to do things. One way of organising the groups could be:

Group A prepares a meal
Group B cooks it
Group C washes up
Group D does the shopping

2   Climbing

3   Duke of Edinburgh Award
This Award was set up to give a challenge to all children, including the physically handicapped. There are three levels of award: Bronze, Silver and Gold. For further information see the Duke of Edinburgh Award Scheme Pamphlet *No Handicap*.

4   Fishing

5   Hill Walking
There are now many nature trails which people in wheel-chairs can follow. As with any walking, suitable clothing is essential, eg good shoes for walkers and good gloves for wheelchair users. The cape from the Artificial Limb and Appliance Centre can be very useful to the wheelchair user.

6   Orienteering
This can be good fun even around a school complex.

7   Riding
For details please contact the Riding for the Disabled Association (address at the end of the book).

8   Ski-ing
To improve balance, a small ski is attached to the bottom of the stick. For details please contact the British Ski Club for the Disabled (address at the end of the book).

9   Swimming
There are two schools of thought: a   no aids should be used but a large number of helpers, ie the Halliwick Method, or b   aids should be used such as arm bands, floats, etc.

Swimming is extremely beneficial to physically handicapped children, particularly as they are often capable of achieving a movement in water that is impossible for them out of it.

Swimming by the Halliwick Method.

Although there is obviously a link between swimming and sport, we consider it a subject in its own right and therefore not within the scope of this book. For competition swimming please contact the British Sports Association for the Disabled Swimming Division (address at the end of the book).

WATER SPORTS
For all water sports, the children should be able to swim fifty metres in light clothing and should wear regulation life jackets approved by the National Schools Sailing Association (British Standards 3595/69).

It is essential that a competent instructor takes control and that he realises the limitations of the children. Capsize drill should always be taught to children about to canoe or sail.

1   Canoeing
There are modified canoes for physically handicapped children.

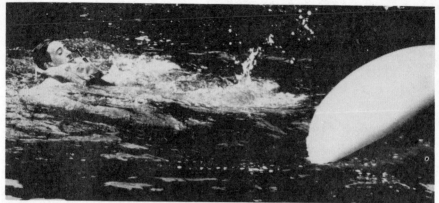

Capsize drill – essential training for canoeing and sailing.

Canoeing.

Modified canoes for physically handicapped children.

2   Dinghy Sailing
Children should never be attached by harness to a boat in case of capsizing.

3   Rowing
For many physically handicapped children, the slides must be fixed. Children should never be harnessed in.

4   Water Polo

5   Water Ski-ing
For details please contact the British Disabled Water Ski Club (address at the end of the book).

ATHLETICS
Suggestions for Organising an Athletics Event for the Disabled.
It is important to bear in mind that as much care and attention to detail are necessary when organising events for the disabled as for the able-bodied. The attitudes that 'the disabled will put up with anything' and that 'they are used to waiting' are ones that we should all make great efforts to eliminate. If a competitor has trained for weeks, he surely merits a well organized event. With this in mind there are a few points to be made:

1   Team leaders must be made to understand that they are responsible for getting all competitors to their events at the appointed time.
2   With track events, the first four or five races should be called together. Following this, as a race is completed, so the next one is called. In this way, while a race is in progress the competitors for the next three races are lined up in their lanes waiting a few yards apart, so that as soon as one race is over the competitors for the next are ready to move up to the starting line. Anyone who is not there on the starting line is disqualified. If this rule is strictly adhered to, the team leaders will make it their business to get their competitors in the right place at the right time and the whole event will run smoothly without interminable waits between the races.
3   This means that the public address system must be clear and ready to operate at the very beginning of the event.
4   It is vital that a clear programme of events is produced and followed.

5 For each race a result card is prepared before the event. One of the judges fills it in as the race finishes and it is taken to the main recorder.

6 The main recorder has a master sheet, also prepared (apart from the winners' names!) before the event. As he is handed the result cards, he enters the results on his master sheet. If there is a house competition or an inter-schools competition, he keeps a running total which he passes on to the master scoreboard. This should be large and clearly visible to all. This helps to maintain the enjoyment of competitors and spectators alike.

7 During the races there should be one person responsible for judging First position, another responsible for Second position, another for Third, and so on. These judges pass on the information to the person filling in the result cards.

8 Each lane has a timer allocated to it. He is responsible for timing the competitor in that lane and passing on the times to whoever is filling in the result card.

9 An independent referee is needed to:
   (i)   Decide on any disputes.
   (ii)   Watch the races and make sure one competitor does not impede another, by going outside his lane.
   (iii) Make sure that all competitors in a walking race are in fact walking.

10 To avoid a child being in a track and a field event at the same time it is usual for wheelchair track events to be going on while the ambulant children do their field events, and vice versa.

11 In the wheelchair dashes the starter should make sure that all the competitors are wearing the regulation calf bands on their wheelchairs which prevent any competitor using his feet to aid propulsion and stop the legs dropping behind the footrests.

12 Any physically handicapped person who takes part in competitive sport run by the British Sports Association for the Disabled needs to be classified according to his handicap. A medical card is filled in by a physiotherapist or a doctor. It is then sent to Stoke Mandeville where each individual is assessed and categorised. The classification may be different for track and field. In any competition the competitor can then enter the relevant race.

Rules
See the official rules for International Stoke Mandeville
Games.

Field Events
Techniques for throwing and the ability to balance will vary
with each individual. The teacher with the physiotherapist
should work out the best technique for each child.

1   *Club*
a   The club is thrown as far as possible within the usual
throwing lines marked on the grass. If the club lands outside
the lines it is a 'no throw'. Competitors must remain seated

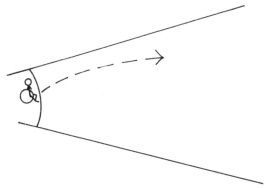

throughout the throw. Anyone who stands on his footplates
half way through the throw is disqualified. The wheelchair
must remain behind the throwing line. The club is thrown
underarm.

b   *Precision Club*

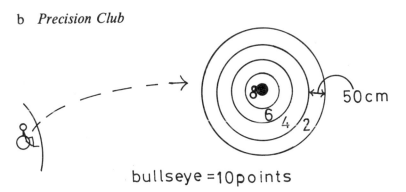

bullseye =10 points

Precision club follows the same rules as 'a' except for the fact that the competitor is aiming at a target marked out on the ground.

2 *Discus*

This is thrown using the usual discus arc marked out on the ground. To build up to throwing the discus horizontally through the air with a spinning action, the children find it useful to start by:

(i)   Rolling the discus along the ground.

(ii)   With a small throw rolling the discus vertically along the ground.

(iii)   Gradually raising the arm to throw the discus vertically through the air.

(iv)   As the arm increases in height, the discus becomes more horizontal (and therefore goes further).

(v)   The discus is finally spun horizontally through the air.

Depending on the individual handicap, it may be advantageous to remove the back and/or the arm of the wheelchair, but remember the child may need to be strapped in. A holding device for wheelchairs may be used, or if this is not available a member of staff may hold the chair.

3 *Javelin*

a   The javelin is thrown within the usual throwing lines marked on the ground. The rules are as for normal javelin throwing, ie:

(i)   The javelin must land within the throwing lines.

(ii)   The point of the javelin must hit the ground first.

As with the discus, the back and/or arm of the wheelchair may need to be removed and the child strapped in. The wheelchair may be held by a member of staff if a holding device for the wheelchair is not available.

b *Precision Javelin*

The same as for javelin except that the child must aim at a target marked on the ground.

c   Instead of a javelin use a basket ball or an even lighter one.

4 *Medicine Ball*

This is thrown by a two handed basketball chest pass throw, as far as possible, within a normal shot put area.

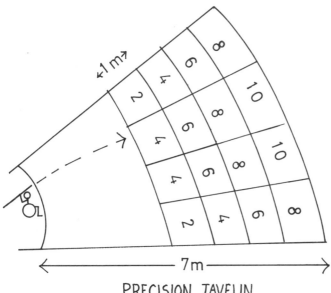

PRECISION JAVELIN

Precision basketball.

5 *Shot*

Use the usual shot put circle marked out on the ground. The rules are as for normal shot putting.

Track Events

More sophisticated sports wheelchairs have been developed and make a significant difference to a competitor's performance. In a recent test it was found that the same child could complete 100 metres six seconds faster in a sports wheelchair than in his own National Health chair. In our view, races should be either for sports wheelchairs or for National Health wheelchairs, for the child who, for whatever reason, has no sports wheelchair is at a decided disadvantage. A very good child in a National Health wheelchair could be beaten by an average child in a sports wheelchair. It is the equivalent of a Formula 1 Grand Prix racing car being allowed to compete against a saloon. Fun and enjoyment should be at the top of the list of priorities, and it can be very disheartening for a child if he fails to get a medal merely because he (or his school) is not fortunate enough to have a good machine. However, given that a sports wheelchair is available, the children must be used to, and happy using it. The wheelchair must be specifically adapted for each individual, which can cause complications if three or four children are using the same wheelchair at the same athletics meeting. Moreover, if a child has not practised in a sports wheelchair he may not be able to guide it and would obviously be better off in his own.

The races are categorised as follows:

a   60 metres dash.
b   100 metres dash.
c   400 metres dash.
d   800 metres dash.
e   1500 metres.
f   *Slalom*

The slalom course is marked out on the ground with various ramps and obstacles to negotiate. There are time penalties if a marker is knocked over, the incorrect course is taken or the competitor falls from his chair. Most able children will manage to negotiate the course with the backs of their wheelchairs down and the arms off for maximum streamlining and manoeuvrability. Some will achieve it on two wheels.

A sports wheelchair.   The 60 metres dash.

g *Relays*

Usually two competitors wait at either end of a 60 metre track. It is necessary to have two lanes per team, for the first competitor comes down one lane and the second one goes up the other, the third follows the first and the fourth the second.

Each competitor must be touched before crossing the starting line (see the International Stoke Mandeville Games Federation Rules).

The Amateur Athletic Association run a Five Star Award Scheme for physically handicapped children. For further details please see the address at the end of the book.

There is also a proficiency scheme for using a wheelchair, details of which may be obtained from the John Jameson School, Leeds.

7 Movement Education

Movement education is essential to the development of the physically handicapped child. In our movement education lessons we aim to train the children to cope with any situation they may find themselves in, within the limitations of their handicap. So that for example, if a child with limited movement fell out of his wheelchair, he would not panic and just lie there in fear until someone came and found him, because he would know that by relaxing and tucking in his head and limbs he could fall without hurting himself. Also that he could move, however unconventionally, the few yards to the telephone to get the necessary help.

How do we train the children to have this confidence in themselves? By putting them in as many situations as possible; by giving them the opportunities to find out what they can do and what it is like to roll, crawl, slither, push, fall, slide, pull, climb, lift, lower, balance, overbalance and so on.

Movement is fundamental to us all. Every one of us has to manage his body weight in a great variety of situations during a typical day. We all have to support and balance our bodies and initiate many different movements which transfer our body weight from one place to another. Moreover we have to do this in relation to other people and things. Thus we have to be aware of our bodies and how they relate to the space around them and the people and things in that space.

Movement and body awareness come naturally to the able-bodied child. As he grows older and progressively ventures out into the wider world, his movement and co-ordination gradually improve. He learns by trial and error what he can and cannot do. His experience teaches him that if his foot goes down a hole, he will fall over unless he takes certain steps to restore his balance. If he runs at speed into a tree, he will hurt himself, and so on.

But often a physically handicapped child does not have any of these experiences. Thus, although movement and body awareness are as vital to his day-to-day living as they are to that of the able-bodied child, they are not naturally assimilated by him as they are by the able-bodied child, perhaps because many people seem to feel that, since the physically handicapped cannot move, their place is in a wheelchair or lying down. They therefore do not have the opportunity of finding out what their bodies can in fact do; nor how their body relates to the space around it, and the people and things in it.

However, if the physically handicapped child is to become at all independent, the two most important things he must find out are just these things – his movement potential and how his body relates to its environment.

To be independent he must, if at all possible, be able to transfer his weight from his bed to a chair, the chair to the lavatory, the chair to a car, the chair to the floor, the floor to the chair, to the bath seat – and so on. Similarly, without body awareness he will find it difficult to dress, to relate to his environment or to be safely left alone.

For these reasons we feel it is essential to teach physically handicapped children to realise their full physical potential and to be confident in their environment – which are the ultimate aims of our movement education lessons.

For the sake of clarity we have divided our movement education into three phases:

1 Pure play
2 Guided play
3 Educational gymnastics

However, we must emphasise that each child must be considered individually and his chronological age is irrelevant.

The three phases are inter-related, and in the lesson situation it is particularly difficult to know when pure play becomes guided play; as a child plays, a suggestion from the teacher/physio guides the child into a new experience, and to an extent his play can now be said to be guided. A few minutes later, however, the child may revert to using his own imagination and to exploring his environment unaided, ie pure play. We therefore feel it is easier to talk about pure play and guided play together. However the teacher/physio must bear in mind that too much guidance can restrict rather than widen. He must not be so eager to widen the child's experience that he represses the child's natural imagination and instincts, thereby causing the child to be inhibited.

When working with young physically handicapped children, one must always remember that it is very likely that they have missed out, as we have already mentioned, on early movement experiences which for the most part come from play which most of us take for granted. If you watch a group of able-bodied infants playing, you will see that they naturally explore the space around them. They crawl, run, jump, fall down, scramble over furniture (when mum's not looking!) climb fences and gates, swing on low branches of trees, climb trees, play in the mud, splash in puddles, and so on. But the average physically handicapped child may have spent most of his time lying on his back or sitting in a wheelchair.

It is therefore up to the teacher/physio to compensate for this, to provide the child with as stimulating an environment as possible and to encourage him to explore it.

PLAY AND GUIDED PLAY

The first thing we do in our movement lesson is to ask all the children to get out of their chairs and onto the floor – if this is at all possible. (There may be the occasional child who is unable to leave his chair for medical reasons). We then do our best to provide them with as many play experiences – albeit in an artificial situation – as possible. We put various pieces of equipment – balls, mats, benches, hoops, trucks, bean bags, and so on – around the room and get the children to explore and encourage them to play. Play is essential, and children who are deprived of it will revert to toddler behaviour at the most inconvenient times when they are older. One boy who came to us as a senior was asked to wash up in a cookery lesson. He spent the afternoon playing in the sink, like a three-year-old. It was his first experience of playing freely with water. So if infants have missed out on the usual play experiences, they must be given the chance to compensate before it is possible to do more specific movement tasks successfully with them.

However there comes a time when the play must be guided. Then the teacher/physio must watch the individual children and try to diversify and develop their play. If the child is doing something which the teacher/physio could follow up, then without imposing a specified activity, the teacher/physio

Moving around on a scooter board.

might make a suggestion to widen the child's experience. For example, a child may be propelling himself on a scooter board. The teacher/physio could suggest that the child might go backwards. Or the teacher/physio might offer a challenge to certain children, for example, to climb up the steps and go down the slide. Or he may create obstacles with benches or mats for the child riding around in a toy train. His aim is continuously to stimulate and widen the child's play experience.

There will no doubt be quite a large range of ability within any one group. Some children will walk confidently and try all manner of things. Some will roll unaided, but there will be some who will need help just to roll over at all. It is often *not* because the child is *physically* incapable of moving but because he has not the confidence to move. If he has always been put in a wheelchair he may be unaware of his physical capabilities. (You only have to observe the difference in two able-bodied children at the swimming pool, to understand the importance of self confidence. The child who has been brought up to go often to the pool will jump straight into the water and play. The other child, confronted with the pool for the first time, will be petrified if he is left at the side and told to jump in).

So with the physically handicapped. Their backgrounds will be as varied as their levels of self confidence and motivation. Thus some will require much more patience, encouragement and practical help than others.

At the Cedar School, the team observe the children and note

Up the steps.

Over the top.

Pose for the camera.

Slide down the other side.

their strengths and weaknesses. Then they have to plan a class programme which will incorporate individual programmes, to develop as fully as possible the skills of each child in the group. To do this they must watch the individuals and see:

1   How mobile each child is.
2   How accustomed he is to thinking for himself, or whether he merely looks around to see what the others are doing.
3   In which ways he moves.
4   How his movement skills could be improved.
5   Whether he is still at the play stage or needs a more defined challenge.

However, the team must also be aware that:

a   Some children have language problems or a lack of language – which will prevent them from understanding instructions.
b   some children have perceptual problems which might prevent them from understanding or putting into practice certain instructions.

It is impossible to tell others how to cope with a particular group because not only is each child different (emotionally, psychologically, motivationally) but each has a different handicap.

We can therefore only suggest ways of encouraging children to move and of developing their movement skills.

The basic points to remember are:

1   The children must learn to be aware of their bodies.
2   The environment must be as stimulating as possible, within the bounds of safety.

1   *Body Awareness*
As explained elsewhere in the book (see page 61) many physically handicapped children are unaware of parts of their body and of their body in relation to the space around it, and to other people and things. They must therefore be *taught* to appreciate the existence of *all* parts of their body and to understand how it relates to other people and things.

2   *A Safe and Stimulating Environment*
When presenting challenges to young children the teacher/ physio should always be safety conscious. Most children will only attempt tasks that are within their capabilities, but

occasionally you will find a child who will attempt a movement which could be potentially dangerous. So the teacher/physio must be aware of the limitations of the children in his group, especially when the children are working off the ground.

Suggestions that may help to develop movement in the physically handicapped child

1 Within the play situation, the teacher/physio should be constantly on the lookout for opportunities to develop the children's awareness of their bodies, to talk about the different parts and to make them understand how one part relates to another, to make up the whole. Games, such as 'Simon Says' (see page 108) can be played. The teacher/physio may see an opportunity to suggest that 'Fred' raises his arm higher or that 'Mary' curls up into a tighter ball.

They will therefore use the opportunity to show 'Fred' that he can reach further than he thinks, or to prove to 'Mary' that she can make herself much smaller.

In this way the children will assimilate facts about themselves.

2 Also within the play situation the teacher/physio can demonstrate to the children that their bodies are divided into:
(i)   bigger parts, ie tummy, back, bottom, side.
(ii) smaller parts, ie elbows, head, feet, knees, hands.
She may then suggest to a child that he should balance (ie remain still) on a big part and then move from one big part of his body to balance on another; then on to another. She may suggest the child balances on one part of his body, then moves so that he is balanced on two parts of his body, then moves again so that he is balanced on four parts of his body. Balance is an extremely important skill for the physically handicapped child to master as far as he can.

3 Still within the play situation, the teacher/physio can introduce the concepts of:
a *Space*, by getting the children to move around the room into a space. Then by getting them to move from one specified spot to another. To turn on the spot.
b *Speed*, by getting a child to move:
(i)   slowly
(ii) as quickly as possible.

c *Direction*, by suggesting the child moves:
    (i)   backwards
    (ii)   forwards
    (iii)   to the right
    (iv)   to the left
    (v)   sideways.

d *Numbers*, by suggesting the children get into pairs, threes or fours.

e *Shape*, by suggesting the child makes a shape with his body – a circle, star, long and narrow, short and fat, like a ball, and so on.

f *Distance*, by suggesting he travels:
    (i)   a short distance
    (ii)   a long distance.

g *Colour*, by specifically asking the child to pick up a red bean bag or a green skittle.

4 Simple equipment can be put into the child's way, such as a ball, bean bags, mats, hoops. Then you can progress to:
'Kick a ball'
'Roll a ball'
'Fetch a ball'
'Roll the ball to a partner'
'Kick the ball to a partner'
'Throw the ball against the wall'
'Throw a bean bag on to a mat'
'Fall on to a mat'
'Bounce a ball.

5 More complicated equipment such as slides, benches, bars, ladders, hammocks, climbing frame, can be introduced. The child can get the experience of swinging in space in a hammock.
'Swing on a ladder or bar'
'Slide or pull yourself along a bench'
'Get on/off a bench or other piece of apparatus'
'Do it quickly or slowly'
'Go over/under a piece of apparatus'
'Get through the polo' (ie a big piece of apparatus shaped like a 'Polo' sweet).

Pull along the bench.

Going over apparatus.

Going under apparatus.

6 Link one movement to another:
'Get on to a bench, pull yourself along it and climb off on the other side.'

Balancing on and off the apparatus is a very important skill to develop. It is also important to teach the children how to handle their bodies should they overbalance. They should be encouraged to balance on as many parts and combinations of

Balancing on the apparatus.

parts of their bodies as possible. If they overbalance they should be encouraged to roll and go with their weight, rather than hit the ground with a big bump.

The movement challenges can often be made more fun by being clothed in imaginative play. For instance, several scooter boards can be joined together to form a train. A child lies on each scooter board and the 'engine' can be asked to go backwards and the 'trucks' to go forwards. Or the children can be giraffes, lifting their heads as high as they can. Let your imagination go! The lessons should be fun and the children should enjoy them.

Enjoyment.

Balancing on three small parts of the body.

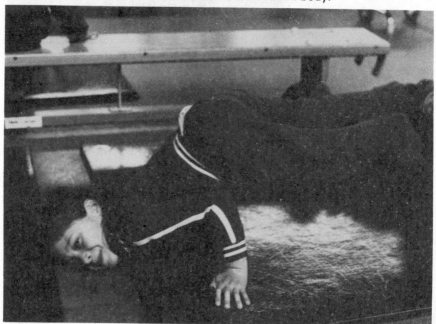

Balancing on a
big part of the
body.

Balancing on small
parts of the body.

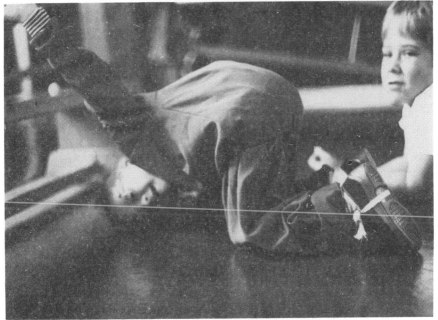

 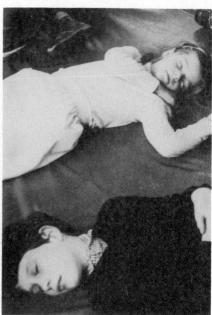

The wizard.   Turned to stone.

We recently took the theme of Hallowe'en. One of the children was the wizard. He had a drum and could cast spells. He turned all the children into frogs, then into monsters. As he banged his drum, the frogs (then monsters) had to move in time to the beat. We then developed another idea from this: that the children should divide into two groups, one of wizards and witches and one of children playing. The wizards and witches mixed up their brews in the corners of the room while the children played in the middle of it. Then the wizards and witches moved towards the children. On a given signal they turned the children into stone. We then asked the wizards and witches for ideas as to what they could turn the children into. They came up with monsters, snakes, birds and so on.

One can develop stories from basic ideas. For example, the teacher/physio says to the children, 'A woodcutter goes into the forest to cut down some trees. As he works a magic bird arrives . . .' From there the teacher/physio builds up a story with the children. The children act it out.

Music can be used to encourage movement. One can develop

Movement can be fun!

a form of keep-fit to music, or adapt 'music and movement' ideas used in ordinary schools. The children respond well to percussion and music, so it should be included in their movement lessons.

Whether the children are 'playing' individually or 'keeping fit to music' in a group it is essential to remember to treat them all as individuals. In this way, each child can use his known movement skills and develop them further *at his own pace*. Each child will therefore achieve at his own level (the praise given by the teacher/physio reinforcing his success). A sense of achievement will boost the child's confidence which in turn will lead to an improved performance.

This however does put an added responsibility on to the teacher/physio. With the emphasis on individual ability and related performance, the teacher/physio by definition must be so aware of his class and their individual capabilities that he will justifiably give praise to the severely handicapped child who performs a simple movement well. But conversely he must be prepared to demand more from the lazy child who cannot be bothered to make the effort – bearing in mind that a playful challenge may get a more positive response than a negative rebuke.

You must always be positive and build on what the children have. Many children do not have a great deal to build on; it is therefore most important to encourage the child to do what he can rather than emphasise the things he cannot do.

When the child has passed through the play experience, he will be ready to face set challenges. It is only when he reaches this point that you should begin to set specific tasks for him to solve. How does one know when a particular child has reached this point? This is the difficult question to answer for it is impossible to generalise. As the teacher/physio watches and gets to know each child, his experience will lead him to know when a child has had enough, or needs a change or a new stimulus or a more exacting challenge. The teacher/physio can then react accordingly. We are very aware that such a statement can be of little help to the inexperienced! Perhaps the only guidelines we can suggest are that the children should enjoy the movement and that there should be a gradual (with some children, a very gradual) improvement in their performance.

The children in the class will almost certainly be at different stages of development. They will therefore need to be grouped. The teacher/physio must also understand that initially some children will need a lot of help and encouragement – not only physical help to perform a task but also verbal suggestions as to how to perform it. Never let a child just lie on the floor and do nothing. A child with very limited movement may need constant individual attention. A lot of helpers are therefore often essential to run the session well.

One very interesting by-product of the movement lessons is the language development and increase in vocabulary and verbal understanding shown by the children. A most important language skill which the movement teacher can develop is the ability to listen and then to follow an instruction.

EDUCATIONAL GYMNASTICS
Many books and guidelines have been produced on the

'modern educational gymnastics' PE lesson, setting out its aims, objectives and content. It is not within the scope of this book to reiterate these, for it is assumed that any teacher who does educational gymnastics with physically handicapped children will have studied the fundamental ideas and will understand what educational gymnastics aim to do.

The physically handicapped child can benefit from educational gymnastics as much as the able-bodied child, and there is no reason why a physically handicapped child should not be included in a lesson with a class of able-bodied children, unless of course the child is barred from doing PE on medical grounds – because of a severe heart condition, for example; the physically handicapped child, like all the able-bodied children, can perform at his own pace and level. Relatively speaking he can be stretched as much as any other child and can achieve as much.

When doing educational gymnastics with a class of physically handicapped children all the themes can be used and adapted, but because of the children's physical and perceptual handicaps a slightly different emphasis is advisable. The following three themes are of paramount importance to the physically handicapped child and should therefore take priority in any movement programme:

1 Weight transference, balance and overbalance.
2 Body awareness.
3 Position in space.

1 Weight Transference and Balance
As there is usually a wide range of physical ability in the children of any class, it is advisable to use less specific terms. So instead of making the request 'run', ask them to move as quickly as possible. Some may run, others may crawl, others roll. Some may merely move from their back to their side (which for a heavily handicapped child would be relatively good and as great a personal achievement as running for another child). Instead of referring to particular parts of the body we use the terms 'small parts and 'large parts', since such open ended terms enable most children to complete a given task. So instead of saying, 'Balance on two legs and two hands' we say, 'Balance on four small parts of the body'. Thus the child who cannot balance on his hands and legs can

balance on his feet and knees or his elbows and hands.

One very important consideration in the early stages of movement education is to teach the child how to cope should he overbalance. To begin with, many of the most severely handicapped children will not be able to get into a position of danger, but for those who can, they should know how to cope if they fall. You can begin by doing a series of preparation exercises on tucking in the small parts of their body, and rounding the large parts. The teacher/physio then asks the child to roll his body into a ball. The teacher/physio can then go round the class and see if it is possible to roll 'the ball'. Then get the children to roll safely from one position into another.

If the child cannot walk, let him get on to the floor. If physically possible, get him to curl up into a rounded position and roll round the floor. Conversely, ask the child to get into a shape which will make it impossible for you to roll him over, eg a star shape. Then discuss the differences in the shapes. Then see if he can move from a rounded shape to an extended shape (ie the star shape). It is especially important for the children to know how to fall if they do exercises off the ground or take part in wheelchair games, or do 'wheelies' (which they love to do).

Some of the children may not be able to move far, but each one can take his weight on some part of his body. From this point of balance every effort should be made to get the child to move to another position of balance. For example, we have a child (with spina bifida) who, when he came to the school, could only move his head, arms and hands – due mainly to the fact that he had always been confined to a wheelchair. So we laid him on the floor on his back. He practised raising his arms towards the ceiling. He then made himself as long as possible by putting his hands above his head on the floor. He next began to be able to get himself on to his side by putting his arms above his head and his head to one side. With a lot of practice he eventually learned to roll. It is now his main means of movement around the floor.

Other ways of transferring weight should be developed – crawling, sliding, twisting, jumping – using as many different parts of the body as possible and in as many different situations as possible. The degree of achievement will vary with each

Transferring weight using apparatus.

child, but it is surprising what many can do with practice and encouragement.

When teaching balance the following are important:

Can the child balance using only small parts of his body?
Can he reduce the balancing base and overbalance into another balance?
Can he move his head and still keep his balance?

Many pieces of apparatus can be used to give the children additional tasks to solve within a movement sequence; for instance a child could be asked to transfer his weight from large parts to small parts of his body then back to large parts, until he comes to a pile of bean bags. He must then select a bean bag and roll towards three hoops (a yellow one, a blue one and green one). He must then place his bean bag in the hoop which matches his bean bag in colour.

2 Body Awareness

Try to get the children to appreciate the existence of all parts of their body, however poor the function of each part may be; for example, a hemiplegic child with little or no use in one side of his body must learn that he can use it to lean on when getting up. Physically handicapped children are often not aware which parts of their body are moving. Many have never seen themselves in a mirror. For this reason we have had several long mirrors (from the floor upwards) placed in the school.

Once a child has seen himself in a mirror, pair children up (children must be of similar ability). One child becomes 'the mirror'. Then the other does an action. The 'mirror' must reproduce it as closely as possible. This helps to teach them how they move.

3 Position in Space

Many physically handicapped children do not have the usual subconscious picture of where their bodies are in space and they will not necessarily pick this up in the normal course of development. They are often not sure where they are in relation to other people.

Bearing in mind that we must always work from the point which the child has reached in his development, a starting point could be his awareness of the ground. Can he balance (remain still) on the ground? Can he get in a line behind someone or next to someone? Can he form a circle with other children? Many at first find such concepts impossible to perceive, but marks on the floor can usually help. If you want the children in a line, a mark at either end can often help them to understand where you want them. Relays can help substantially.

We have tried to give ideas for the three themes which are of greatest importance in the movement lessons. However any themes can be used, as in educational gymnastic lessons for the able-bodied.

But just as the three themes cited are of particular importance to the movement development of the physically handicapped child, so some themes are difficult to use or may even be impossible for some children. One which comes to mind is that of flight. Many are unable to jump. They can however get the experience of swinging in space if they are put in a hammock.

When using any theme it can be made more interesting by introducing:
a   Variations in speed. A task may be completed slowly/in a sustained way/suddenly/quickly/very quickly.

Playing individually
on the climbing
frame.

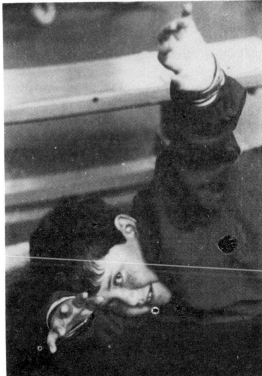

As high as possible.

b   Different levels – as high as possible/as low as possible/ changing from one level to another.

c   Variations in directions – forwards/backwards/sideways/ diagonally/upwards/downwards.

d   Variation in the degree of sensitivity – twist gently/jump strongly.

e   Variation in the path – go straight to a given point/take an indirect path/go in a zig-zag path to a given point.

With physically handicapped children as with the able-bodied, one is ideally working towards the movement lesson which starts with a warming up session, followed by a period of floor work, followed by apparatus work – all based on a theme.

With some groups of children this is possible, but do not despair if others never seem to progress beyond the guided play stage. Like able-bodied children, some will develop more than others and will achieve more. So many factors are involved besides the physical handicap. But one has achieved a great deal with the children if they enjoy their movement lessons and if one is able to develop the movement potential of each child to its full.

Wheelchair Dancing
Wheelchair dancing can be a great source of fun and enjoyment. It also helps the participant to develop:

a   A sense of rhythm

b   An awareness of his position in space.

c   A precise manoeuvring of his wheelchair.

Wheelchair dancing.

8 What of the Future?

We hope that this book has proved useful to all those who deal with sport for the physically handicapped. We also hope that we have given some inspiration to those who are trying to integrate a physically handicapped child into an ordinary school. We especially hope that we have shown that the physically handicapped child has a lot to offer and does not necessarily need to while away the games lesson in the library.

How do we see the future? The future for the physically handicapped school leaver and of sport for the physically handicapped?

Given the present high unemployment situation, it is very likely that the physically handicapped school leaver will have difficulty in finding either full or part-time employment. The opportunities open to him are few. If he cannot get a job, then he can either go to a sheltered workshop, to a further education college, or stay at home.

Whatever he does, sport can be of immense value to him. For not only will it give him the opportunity to maintain the fitness and independence he gained at school, but also it can extend his social contact and give him an absorbing interest.

What opportunities for sport are open to the physically handicapped person once he or she leaves school?

1 There may be a local British Sports Association for the Disabled Club (see address at the back of the book). These hold sporting competitions and also run social events.

2 There are also Physically Handicapped and Able Bodied clubs (see address at the back of the book) which aim to combine the talents of the able-bodied and the physically handicapped. These clubs hold many competitive, social and fund-raising events.

3 There are many able-bodied clubs which would welcome

the physically handicapped, for in certain sports they can often compete on equal terms with the able-bodied. For example, bowls, archery, pistol and rifle shooting, pétanque (see addresses at the back of the book). However the physically handicapped must have the courage to go and ask to join since the able-bodied in the club probably have not given the handicapped a thought – not because they do not want to but because nobody has made them aware of their existence.

4 Most swimming pools encourage handicapped members.

5 New leisure centres provide facilities for competition and relaxation with:

    a swimming pools
    b basketball halls
    c table tennis
    d volley ball
    e badminton
    f indoor archery

and many other recreational activities, together with a social life.

However, once the physically handicapped person has decided to join a particular club, which may not have been specifically designed for the disabled, he may have to overcome difficult problems of access and general facilities. If he is to retain his independence there must be a ramp and double doors where necessary. Many handicapped people need a low changing bench, the size of a bed, in order to be able to change unaided. Although such items of furniture are fairly simply installed, the problem of access can present far greater difficulties. But it would seem that many clubs are prepared to make a great effort to ensure their buildings are accessible to the disabled once they realise the benefits that the physically handicapped can derive from their sport. One good example known to us is a local bowling club – the Atherley, in Southampton. Some of their members took a group of our senior children and taught them to bowl to a standard which enabled the children to compete at national level and win. We hope that some of our school leavers will be able to join their club. Initially access posed quite a problem, but when the club had an extension built, a ramp and double doors were included to make the building, and therefore the club, completely accessible.

Changes which could improve sport for the physically handicapped

1 On the one hand there seems to be a great deal of ignorance among the general public concerning the disabled. On the other, many physically handicapped people seem to be inhibited in the presence of able-bodied people. This unhappy situation can only be remedied by constant contact between the two, which will generate more understanding and awareness generally.

At the moment there is very little publicity given to sporting events involving the physically handicapped. The media could do much to remedy this. Perhaps the new TV channel will have a more enlightened approach and we shall soon see more sports for the physically handicapped televised. Anyone who has ever been to a good wheelchair basketball game cannot but be impressed by the atmosphere which is generated. It is no less electric than that which emanates from a game played by the able-bodied. The competition is as tough and the game as enjoyable. In fact, the game can often be more interesting, given the extra skills required to manoeuvre a wheelchair and handle the ball at one and the same time.

2 The structure of competitive sport for the physically handicapped is the same as for the able-bodied. There are inter-school competitions, inter-county, inter-regional, national and every four years the Olympic Games. However, we should like to see sports for the disabled incorporated into the able-bodied sports events, at local, county, regional and national levels, for we can see no advantage in running the two events as separate entities. It may be argued that the organisation would be far too complicated, but in our view the benefits gained by *all* participants would more than compensate for the small increase in administration caused by the inclusion of additional classes for the disabled.

3 If the disabled classes were included in the able-bodied events from local to national level, it would mean that entry to major competitions would be standardised. The physically

handicapped competitor would start at the local event and gradually win through to national level, as does the able-bodied competitor – with the kudos and excitement this brings. Moreover the disabled would be as proud as able-bodied children to represent their country, if they were given the opportunity. At the moment entry is not standardised for the physically handicapped. At the National Games for the handicapped a school like the Cedar School is at present competing against regional teams (such as the North Regional) or national teams (such as the Welsh team). Although we choose to do this it is because the alternative is not to compete at all in the Stoke Mandeville National Junior Games – which would mean our children would miss out altogether.

4   We also feel that the classification system necessary for physically handicapped sportsmen needs to be reviewed. For example, a high lesion spina bifida may look just like a paraplegic, so they are often put in the same class. They both have paralysed limbs and both are sitting in a wheelchair; there, however, the similarity often ends. The spina bifida competitor has many more problems to overcome before he can score the goal that the paraplegic finds relatively easy. He often has severe perceptual problems and more complex physical problems in addition to his paralysis. Moreover, the paraplegic whose paralysis is the result of an accident later on in life, still has the wealth of experience acquired before his accident. The spina bifida lacks this, which must put him at a disadvantage. For these reasons we feel it is necessary to reconsider whether the two can justifiably be placed in the same class.

5   The present classification system runs from Wheelchair/ Ambulant One to Wheelchair/Ambulant Five. This works well in itself, but in practice there is little opportunity for the groups four and five to compete at a higher level than school. They can enjoy competitive sport at their own level as much as the top two classes; there should therefore be the opportunity for schools to enter the severely handicapped at regional and national levels. It might take a little time to get started because at the moment it is traditional to concentrate on the classes one and two. But once it was realised how much classes four and five could benefit from and enjoy competition, it would soon catch on.

6   We would suggest that events such as flik ball games, shuffle board (see page 116) and Unihoc could be very much enjoyed by the classes four and five. More of these events could well be included in the regional and national games.

7   The benefits gained from team games are many. Schools offer a variety of such games as part of the sports curriculum, but only basketball is offered to our children at regional or national level. Basketball played totally to able-bodied rules exempts all but the wheelchair one classified children, and so relatively few children have the opportunity to compete in team sports. However, as we have tried to show, there are many exciting team games which can be played by the physically handicapped. Could some of these not be encouraged at regional and national level?

8   We also feel that it is important to grade *all* sports for the physically handicapped. At the moment table tennis is nationally and regionally an open competition. This means that a dystrophy boy can never hope to get a medal, for however good he is in his own class, he cannot possibly hope to win against a paraplegic. Again we are sure that if the competition were graded nationally and regionally it would encourage the more severely handicapped to take part. As long as the competition is open most of them obviously will not enter.

9   As explained on page 126, we feel it is important to have races *either* for sports wheelchairs *or* for National Health wheelchairs. It is so disappointing for a child who has practised hard in a National Health wheelchair, and who has become very proficient, to lose a race to a better machine rather than a better performer.

10   Finally, we would make a plea on behalf of all physically handicapped people to the architects and planners and organisers of sports stadia to give a thought to the disabled.
    The physically handicapped identify with professional sportsmen as much as their able-bodied peers. They follow the local football team with as much loyalty and enthusiasm – only to find that often they are unable to watch their team at first hand unless someone carries them into the stadium and they sit on a most uncomfortable seat. The physically handicapped

A game at the Dell.

have their self-respect and pride, and it takes a lot of courage for a hefty muscular dystrophy to be wheeled into the stadium to wait until someone gets the message and offers to carry him to his seat. Yet we have seen this situation at Wembley Stadium – the country's largest sports stadium. It was also a major operation for us – and we took several strong helpers! – when we took a group of our children to a Cup Final there, for the stairs make access in a wheelchair impossible. All the children had to be bodily carried. The staff were very friendly and extremely helpful in carrying the children to their seats, but it should not have been necessary; with a little thought and care the stadium could be modified to accommodate wheelchairs. In our view it would also make it very much safer in the event of fire or the need to clear the stadium quickly.

The Cedar School has had a lot of contact with our local football team, Southampton (the 'Saints'), and with individual players of the calibre of Alan Ball and Steve Moran who have both refereed house matches and sports day competitions. Several times groups of children have been invited to the Dell (the team's ground) to talk to and watch the players train, and even to take them on, on a full size pitch with a full size goal! The children involved got such a thrill from the experience – as any football enthusiast would.

Southampton have now modified their ground to make wheelchair access possible, so the physically handicapped in the area have the same opportunity as anyone else to watch their favourite team.

Sporting bodies are becoming more aware of the need to ensure wheelchair access. At the Dell they have proved it is possible to modify existing stadia, but there are still far too many sporting venues (Wembley being a case in point) where the physically handicapped are denied the opportunity of spectating and of first hand enjoyment because wheelchair access is impossible.

To conclude, it is our experience that sport can be as important in the life of the physically handicapped child as in that of his able-bodied peer. He can enjoy participating just as much, and within the limit of his handicap he can also achieve as much. He can enjoy identifying with the professionals with equal enthusiasm and he can be just as eager to watch.

We only hope that we have managed to convince our readers of our beliefs and to inspire them enough to give our ideas a try, so that the physically handicapped child will no longer be left propped in a wheelchair as an under achiever, but will rather be encouraged to discover how much he can do, with the feeling of fulfilment that endeavour can bring.

Appendix

LIFTING

General Notes

To prevent accidents and misuse of your body and to make the job as easy as possible, it is wise to lift correctly.

1 The leg muscles are the strongest and most powerful in the body. Use these to lift, and not the weaker back muscles.

2 A well performed lift starts to move the object forwards as well as upwards.

3 Lift with your feet apart to give you a well balanced position – usually one in front of the other.

4 In the starting position, knees and hips should be fully bent, with back and head as straight as possible and with chin tucked in.

5 Keep the object you are lifting as close to you as possible.

6 Make a smooth, co-ordinated and controlled lift keeping the back straight – no sudden jerks.

7 Breathe out at the time of maximum effort.

8 When lifting a heavy object, if help is available, use it!!

Lifting Children

1 Poorly executed lifts are uncomfortable and embarrassing for the children being lifted.

2 All the general rules given above apply.

3 Any child with weak shoulder muscles must be lifted without straining or dislocating his shoulders. For example:

   a Child crosses arms across chest.

   b You thread your arms either side of his chest and firmly grasp his forearms.

   c Pressure when lifting should be of your forearms on his rib cage, not upwards through his shoulders.

4 With two lifters, the procedure for the one lifting the top part of the child's body is as 3. The lifter on the 'legs' keeps the

child's knees together whilst supporting underneath to prevent strained muscles.

5 If the child is to be lifted from floor to chair with a small amount of leg power and only one lifter:

   a Lifter grasps as 3.
   b Child sitting on floor with knees drawn up.
   c Lifter positioned as with general rules.
   d Rock child forward onto feet.
   e Re-position your feet as necessary.
   f Lift either to chair or to standing.

USEFUL ADDRESSES

1 Association for Spina Bifida and Hydrocephalus, (ASBAH), 30 Devonshire Street, London W1N 2EB. Tel: 01-935 9060/01-486 6100.

2 Scottish Spina Bifida Association, 190 Queensferry Road, Edinburgh, EH4 2BW. Tel: 031-332 0743.

3 Spastics Society, 12 Park Crescent, London W1N 4EQ. Tel: 01-636 5020.

4 Scottish Council for Spastics, Rhuemore, 22 Corstorphine Road, Edinburgh, EH12 6HP. Tel: 031-337 2804/2616.

5 Muscular Dystrophy Group of Great Britain, Nattrass House, 35 Macaulay Road, Clapham, London SW4 0QP. Tel: 01-720 8055. *and* 26 Borough High Street, London SE1 9QG.

6 Haemophilia Society, PO Box 9, 16 Trinity Street, London SE1 1DE. Tel: 01-407 1010.

7 Brittle Bone Society, 63 Byron Crescent, Dundee, DD3 6SS. Tel: Dundee (0382) 87130.

8 British Epilepsy Association, 3–6 Alfred Place, London WC1E 7ED. Tel: 01-580 2704.

9 Scottish Epilepsy Association, 48 Goran Road, Glasgow G51 1JL. Tel: 041-427 4911.

10 Cystic Fibrosis Research Trust, 5 Blythe Road, Bromley, Kent, BR1 3RS. Tel: 01-464 7211.

11 Association for Children with Heart Disorders, 536 Colne Road, Reedley, Nr. Burnley, Lancs. Tel: Burnley (0282) 27500.

12 British Heart Foundation, 57 Gloucester Place, London WC1H 4DH. Tel: 01-935 0185.

13   Disabled Living Foundation,
     346 Kensington High Street, London W14 8NG. Tel:
     01-602 2491.

14   Central Council for the Disabled,
     34 Ecclestone Square, London, SW14 1PE. Tel: 01-821
     1871.

15   Central Council for Physical Recreation,
     70 Brompton Road, Knightsbridge, London SW3 1EX.

16   Wales Council for the Disabled,
     Crescent Road, Caerphilly, Mid Glamorgan. Tel: (0222)
     869 224.

17   Football Association (Super Skills) Award Scheme,
     22–24a The Broadway, Darkes Lane, Potters Bar, Herts.

18   Grand National Archery Society,
     c/o 20 Broomfield Road, Chelmsford, Essex.

19   Angling – National Anglers Council,
     c/o Flat D, St George's Lodge, Muswell Hill, Hornsey,
     London N10 3TE.

20   Athletics – Amateur Athletic Association,
     c/o Sports Council, 70 Brompton Road, Knightsbridge,
     London SW3 1EX.

21   English Schools Athletics Association,
     c/o 26 Conscliffe Road, Stanley, Tyne and Wear, DH9
     7RF.

22   Badminton Association of England,
     44–45 Palace Road, Bromley, Kent, BR1 3JU.

23   British Sports Association for the Disabled,
     Hayward House (Sir Ludvig Guttman Sports Centre),
     Stoke Mandeville, Harvey Road, Aylesbury, Bucks HP21
     8PP.

24   English Basketball Association,
     Calomax House, Lupton Avenue, Leeds LS9 7DD.

25   English Bowling Association,
     150 Wellington Road, Enfield, Middlesex EW1 2RH.

26 Canoeing – British Canoe Union,
70 Brompton Road, Knightsbridge, London SW3 1EX.

27 Duke of Edinburgh Award,
5 Prince of Wales Terrace, London W8 5PG.

28 Handball,
38 Lea Road, Hoddesdon, Herts.

29 Les Autres,
c/o Stoke Mandeville Sports Stadium, Harvey Road,
Aylesbury, Bucks.

30 Orienteering Federation,
3 Oakbank House, Skelsmergh, Kendal, Cumbria.

31 British Pétanque for the Disabled,
Mr R. Page, 58a Freeground Road, Hedge End, Southampton, Hants.

32 PHAB (Physically Handicapped and Able-Bodied),
42 Devonshire Street, London W1N 1LN. Tel: 01-637
7475.

33 British Ski Club for the Disabled,
14 Easton Street, High Wycombe, Bucks.

34 Association of Swimming Therapy,
24 Arnos Road, London N11.

35 British Disabled Water Ski Association,
Mrs Maere D. Edge, Warren Wood, The Warren,
Ashtead, Surrey KT21 2SN.

36 National Wheelchair Dance Association,
8 Starvecrow Close, Shipbourne, Tonbridge, Kent, TN11
9NW.

BOOK LIST

Physical Education for the Physically Handicapped, Department of Education and Science, London HM Stationery Office, 1971.

Physical Education for Children with Special Needs, Lillian Groves, Cambridge University Press, 1979.

Physiotherapy in Paediatric Practice, David Scrutton & Moyra Gilbertson, Postgraduate Paediatric Series, Butterworth, 1975.

No Handicap to Dance, Gina Levete, Human Horizons Series, Souvenir Press, 1982.

Textbook of Sport for the Disabled, Sir Ludwig Guttman, CBE, FRS, MD, FRCP, FRCS, HM & M Publishers, 1976.

Outdoor Adventure for Handicapped People, Mike Cotton, Human Horizons Series, Souvenir Press, 1983.

Out of Doors with Handicapped People, Mike Cotton, Human Horizons Series, Souvenir Press, 1981.

Outdoor Pursuits for Disabled People, Norman Croucher, Disabled Living Foundation, 1974.